Computing
&
ICT Lesson Plans

for the Primary School

First published 2017

By Will Fastiggi
Website: www.technologyforlearners.com

Contents

About the Author

Will Fastiggi started his teaching career as a classroom teacher in a large inner-city London primary school. After more than a decade of teaching, Will has worked in schools in the UK, China, Guatemala, El Salvador, and most recently, Brazil.

Graduating with a Masters in Digital Technologies, Communication & Education from the University of Manchester, Will has worked as a teacher, trainer and ICT Coordinator. He has a keen interest in developing the Computing & ICT curriculum in primary education and making practical use of digital technologies for schools.

Currently, Will is an Upper Primary Coordinator and ICT teacher at The British School in Rio de Janeiro. You can find out more about Will from his blog, **technologyforlearners.com**.

Publisher's Acknowledgements

Screenshots of applications (e.g. Purple Mash, Microsoft Publisher and Scratch) used with permission. In some instances, I have been unable to trace the owners of copyright material for images and would appreciate any information that would enable me to do so.

Foreword on the Curriculum

The lesson plans provided in this book are aligned with the expectations outlined under the National Curriculum for England, and at the same time can easily be adapted to an international context. In fact, all of the lessons featured here have been tried and tested successfully in the classroom within an international setting, running concurrently with the International Primary Curriculum (IPC).

The name "computing" reflects the rebranding of the former subject ICT as of 2014 when there was a shift of focus towards computer science in English schools. For the purpose of this book though, I decided to keep "ICT" in the title to emphasise that these plans can also cater for lessons involving information communication technologies, which permeate across the whole school curriculum.

That said, the focus on computer science is what sets computing apart from ICT. This explains why much of the media attention around the world given to this subject has focused increasingly on children 'learning to code'. It is worth mentioning however, that whilst 'coding' is an important skill, which this book certainly helps to develop in the primary years, computing is not just about computer science, and computer science is not just about coding. Although computer science is at the core of computing, this book also includes plenty of lessons and ideas to develop students' learning of information technology and digital literacy. As well as encouraging the use of desktop computers, laptops and iPads, various other digital resources and peripheral devices are recommended throughout this book to help enhance the quality of lessons.

Many countries teach programming in secondary schools, but England was the first country in the world to do so in the primary school from the age of five up. Digital technology is a significant part of all our lives nowadays, so understanding how it works ought to be an entitlement for all. In doing so, more children can go on to become creators of digital technology rather than just passive users. Whether you are teaching in England or overseas, this book is sure to provide you with a wealth of engaging lessons for your students.

Introduction

This book is a compilation of lesson plans for Computing & Information Communication Technology (ICT) lessons for use by teachers in the primary school. Designed to be used with students from 5 to 11 years, Computing & ICT Lesson Plans for the Primary School contains exciting, challenging and academically relevant lessons for all children at primary age who use computers in school. This book does assume a certain level of subject specific knowledge on the part of teachers. Nevertheless, all the lesson plans provided are very easy to follow, and as long as the specified applications are installed on the computers, this book serves as an excellent pick up and go resource for teachers, curriculum coordinators and administrators.

In terms of curriculum content, computer science is at the core of many of these lesson plans, in which students are taught the principles of computation, how digital systems work, and how to put this knowledge to use through programming. Building on this understanding, students are equipped to use information technology to create content using a variety of software. This book also ensures that students develop digital literacy – able to use, and express themselves and develop their ideas through ICT – as active participants in a digital world. There is a particular focus for example, on Digital Citizenship and E-Safety, so for every year group dedicated lesson plans are provided for these topics.

A differentiated metric of Beginning, Developing and Mastering success criteria (adopted from the International Primary Curriculum's Assessment for Learning programme) is used, which is available to view on the lesson plans at the start of each unit. Progress can then be assessed both formatively and summatively based on this criteria. As students move into Upper Primary (Year 5 & 6 / 9 to 11 years old), it is recommended that they create digital portfolios using Google Sites in which to showcase their learning. In addition, the other productivity tools provided by Google Apps for Education, such as Docs, Sheets & Slides are very useful, as they provide students with many ways in which to collaborate and showcase their learning.

Other key software recommendations include the web-based applications, Purple Mash (available on subscription) and Scratch (free both online and offline), which form the basis of many different lessons in this book. For video editing, a free software such as Windows Movie Maker can be a valuable introduction for children learning to create their own videos. Likewise, GIMP (also free) or Affinity Photo (previously PhotoPlus, available for purchase) serve as great photo editing tools. An IT management software such as NetSupport, which is used to remote control computers in the lab setting, can be a useful addition to help facilitate lessons. Although these particular applications and others referenced in this book come as recommended, technology is constantly changing and other applications may work equally well to help students fulfil the learning objectives outlined in this book. The most important thing is to ensure that students get a thorough grounding in the knowledge, skills and understanding of the digital technology itself.

This is an exciting time to teach Computing & ICT. By delivering the ambitious program of study presented through the lessons in this book, you will be helping to develop your students' knowledge, skills and understanding across the Computing & ICT curriculum, which will prepare them well for the all-encompassing digital sphere of 21st century life!

Recommended Resources

Although these additional resources presented here are not necessary, they make lessons more engaging and help a lot with students' development of key Computing and ICT skills:

Bee-Bots are sturdy robots with four directional keys (forward, back, left and right). Children have to think about where they want the Bee-Bot to go and then input a sequence of directions using the directional keys. Pressing the green GO button then gets the Bee-Bot moving in 6" steps and 90 degree turns. Used with Bee-Bot mats, which feature a grid layout, children learn to use directional language and can begin to understand the concept of programming in terms of a sequence of instructions.

Cubetto is a wooden robot that comes with a wooden interface board (the remote-control unit) in which to place colourful blocks and a fabric grid map. Each of the plastic blocks represents a different directional instruction (forward, left, right and function). As the children insert the blocks into the slots on the board, they create a "queue" of instructions, which are executed as soon as the blue "Go" button is pressed on the interface board. By placing a sequence of blocks onto the interface board, children are building and can see a chain of sequential instructions in a "queue", as the robot executes the instructions in order. As with the Bee-Bots, children can begin to understand the concept of a program as a sequence of instructions to be carried out. However, the advantage of the Cubetto over the Bee-Bot is that the Cubetto's sequence of instructions is visible.

The **Dash & Dot robots** provide an entertaining introduction to the world of programming for younger children. Created by Wonder Workshop, the robots are already fully assembled on purchase but require one of currently five different possible iPad apps in order to play. By interacting with the world around them via sensors, Dash & Dot can hear sounds, detect objects, and respond if you are moving them. The iPad apps then enable you to program these robots to do virtually anything you want, including the delivery of messages, playing musical instruments and navigating obstacle courses.

The **Intuos Draw Wacom Tablet** is the perfect tool for starting out in digital art. A pressure-sensitive stylus (pen) is included with each tablet that makes drawing and painting feel natural, just like using a pen on paper. As anyone who has tried drawing with a mouse will know, it is difficult to produce a decent piece of artwork when you can only use dragging motions that require your entire hand. A mouse is ideal when it comes to navigating the web for example, but when you want to create artwork on the screen with precision, a pen tablet gets you noticeably better results. Using the software, ArtRage Lite, which comes free with the Wacom pen tablet, students are able to blend colours, add effects, and apply retouching effects easily. This all helps to create digital artwork that looks more natural than could otherwise be achieved using just a mouse.

Osmo is a unique application and gaming accessory for the iPad. Along with the four apps (Tangram, Numbers, Words and Newton), each kit comes with a reflector and stand. The reflector slots over the iPad's front-facing camera so that the accompanying apps can see what is on a surface directly in front of the screen. In this way, the technology bridges the physical and digital worlds – each Osmo app allows the user to move physical pieces around in front of the iPad's screen. Unlike many other apps on the market, this novel feature alone means that several children can be using the same iPad at once. It is therefore a great kit for promoting collaboration and teamwork among students.

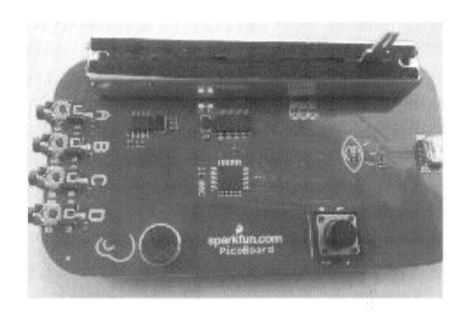

The **PicoBoard** is a piece of hardware that allows Scratch projects to interact with the outside world. The circuit boards contain several sensors (including sound, light and motion), which enable students to create some very imaginative programs in Scratch. It is also a valuable resource in order to challenge students to solve programming problems.

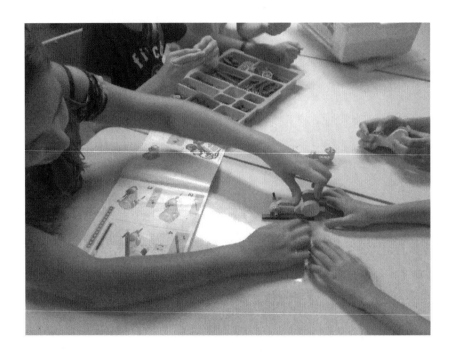

Lego Mindstorm is a robotics construction set that provides learners with a fun, practical approach to learning computer programming. Included in each set (whichever version you get) is a 'brick' computer that controls the system, a set of sensors and motors, as well as Lego parts to create the mechanical system. Once built, the students can connect the robots to computers via USB, which can then start to be programmed using the Lego Mindstorm NXT software. The software is easy to use, as it is very visual, includes lots of video tutorials and provides clear instructions on how to get the robot to do different things. As the children learn to program the robots to perform simple tasks, they can chop and change the code in order to get the robots to perform increasingly complex actions, involving a range of different movements, sounds and images on the screen.

Makey Makeys turn anything that conducts electricity into a remote control, making these tools brilliant for teaching students about electrical circuits. The kit includes the Makey Makey circuit board itself, alligator clips and a USB cable. When the circuit is complete and all the alligator clips are connected, via the Makey Makey board, to something that conducts electricity, an everyday item (for example, a banana, as appears on the front cover of this book) serves as a button on the keyboard!

3D Printer Pens rapidly melt and then cool plastic filament, enabling students to literally draw in 3D. Fun to use, these pens are perfect for any unit related to design. Various models are available - the GooDoo model pictured here is relatively inexpensive, reliable and comes with 20 metres of plastic filament. Having to use this tool meticulously in order to get the desired results is also a good exercise in concentration, patience and tenacity!

Year 1 – Digital Citizenship

Assessment focus area: Digital Literacy & Information Technology

Beginning (**Must**)	Developing (**Should**)	Mastering (**Could**)
Listen to a story.	Give reasons why it is important to ask for help when using the Internet sometimes. Practice putting name and date on something they produce.	Identify examples of good and bad behaviour online. Send work to the printer. Save and retrieve work.

Lesson 1 & 2: Understand the importance of asking for help from an adult when using the Internet
Lesson 3: Identify good behaviour online

Lesson 1 & 2
Understand the importance of asking for help from an adult when using the Internet

Note to teacher: This lesson is from Childnet International and full details of the plan can be found on the web page (www.childnet.com/resources/smartie-the-penguin). The first part of this lesson can be delivered in the classroom because it simply involves reading the children a story about Smartie and asking questions. This should should take about half an hour. The second part of the lesson (the activity) follows up on the story and should be completed in the lab.

Introduction
Explain to the children that they are going to be thinking about the Internet and different types of technology.
Start by asking some simple 'show-of-hand' questions:
Who has used a computer/laptop at home?
Who has a tablet at home, or has played on one?
Who likes to play games online?
Who has an Xbox / Wii / Nintendo DS / PSP / PlayStation etc.?
Who has been on the internet before?
What are their favourite websites and why do they like them?

Present the story of Smartie the Penguin utilising the resources available at http://www.childnet.com/resources/smartie-the-penguin. Make sure to invite the children to contribute their answers when the "Time to Chat" questions come up.

After reading the story, demonstrate for the children how to log into Purple Mash, which can be found on the school Intranet > Students > Purple Mash (https://www.purplemash.com/login/default/launch?launchurl= %2F). Explain that they will use their login badge, which you will hand out once they are ready to go on to the computers. Model for the children how to access 2Paint.

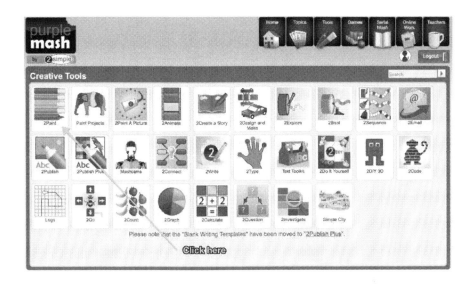

Activity

Using 2Paint, the children should recreate a picture of Smartie the Penguin. As an extension, ask the children to type their names at the bottom left hand side of the screen.

Smartie the Penguin

Plenary

Recap on the story of Smartie the Penguin. What did the children learn? Why is it important to ask for help if we are unsure?

Lesson 3
Identify good behaviour online

Introduction

Discuss with the children why it is important to treat others respectfully. Explain that this is also important when we are using the Internet.

Show this video about how to treat others online:
https://www.youtube.com/watch?v=0u6-2aCea-M

Then direct the children to the feelings application in Paint Projects:

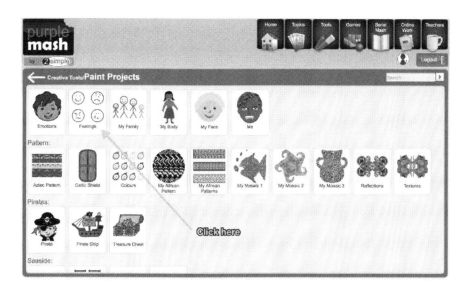

Activity

Children will use the feelings application to create an image for four different feelings: happy, sad, angry and scared.

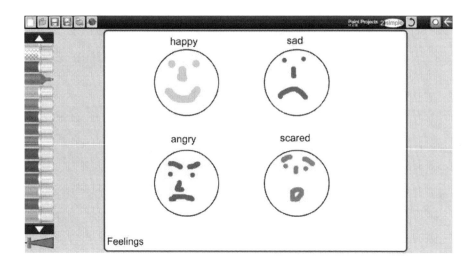

Plenary

Ask the children in what situations they might have these feelings when using the computer. Discuss what they should do in each situation.

Year 1 - Drawing

Assessment focus area: Digital Literacy & Information Technology

Beginning (**Must**)	Developing (**Should**)	Mastering (**Could**)
Log into Purple Mash.	Make several different drawings, using a range of tools.	Send work to the printer. Save and retrieve work.

Lesson 1: Use iPad to make a drawing
Lesson 2: Complete a Paint Project using Purple Mash
Lesson 3: Create a picture using 2Paint
Lesson 4: Use Mashcam tool to create a character display
Lesson 5: Make a picture using 2Paint a Picture
Lesson 6: Use shape and fill tools

Lesson 1
Use iPad to make a drawing

Introduction
Introduce children to iPad app, Draw Free. Show the children the different colour background that they can choose, as well as the different pen and brush types. Demonstrate how to use the colour fill tool. Ask children to draw a picture of their favourite toy.

Activity
Children go ahead and make a picture using Draw Free.

Plenary
Using the Air Server application on the iPads, showcase selected examples of children's work. What effects worked well? What could be improved?

Lesson 2
Complete a Paint Project using Purple Mash

Introduction
Demonstrate for the children how to log into Purple Mash, which can be found on the school Intranet > Students > Purple Mash (https://www.purplemash.com/login/default/launch?launchurl=%2F). Explain to the children that they will use their login badge, which you will hand out once they are ready to go off to the computers.

Show the children the Paint Projects application on Purple Mash. Explore a few examples with the children. Ask the children to choose one of the paint projects to work on.

Activity
Using Purple Mash, children choose a paint project to create their own picture.

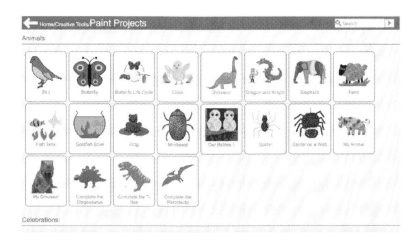

Plenary
Children should save their work. Collect in the login badges, ready to hand out again next lesson.

Lesson 3
Create a picture using 2Paint

Introduction

Remind children how to log into Purple Mash, which can be found on the school Intranet > Students > Purple Mash (https://www.purplemash.com/sch/bsrdj). Explain again to the children that they will use their login badge, which you will hand out once they are ready to go off to the computers.

Model clicking on 2Paint. You can show the video tutorial (look at the video icon on the top right-hand side). Demonstrate using the different brush tools and colours to draw a picture of yourself. When finished, model how to save the image (as shown below).

Activity

Using their login badges, children go ahead and access 2Paint. They should draw a picture of themselves using the different paint tools available. As an extension, the children should design a background for their image.

Plenary
Make sure all the children save their work. Using NetSupport, share examples of children's work with the rest of the class. Collect in the login badges, ready to hand out again next lesson.

Lesson 4
Use Mashcam tool to create a character display

Introduction
Introduce children to the Mashcam tool on Purple Mash. Show them how to take a photo of themselves using the webcam (students will need to click on the icon of a camera).

Activity
Students log onto Purple Mash and click on Mashcam. Using this tool, students should choose a character and then take a photo of themselves using the webcam. Once this has been done, they should write about themselves in the speech bubble.

As an extension, students can record a message about themselves using the record button.

Plenary

Children can save and print their work once they have finished.

Lesson 5
Make a picture using 2Paint a Picture

Introduction
Show the children how to access 2Paint a Picture application from Purple Mash. Explain to the children that they have more options with this app to produce different styles of painting depending on the paint brush they use. Go over some examples, including Swirly, Impressionism and Splash.

Activity
Children should use 2Paint a Picture application to create a digital painting using a range of different brush styles.

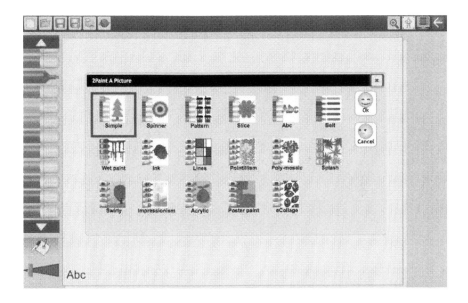

Plenary
Make sure children save their work when they have finished. Showcase some examples of children's work for the rest of the class using NetSupport.

Lesson 6
Use shape and fill tools

Introduction
Show the children how to access Microsoft Paint. Model how to use the shape tool to create different shapes. Then show how to use the fill tool to colour in the shapes.
Demonstrate saving the image (File > Save As), typing a name, e.g. My Image.

Activity
Children should produce a self-portrait using the range of shapes and colour options available. As an extension, they can add a background to this self-portrait.

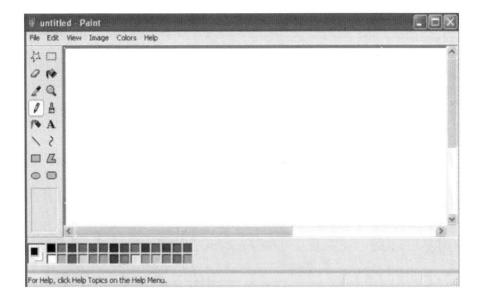

Plenary
Ask children to save their image. Those who have finished can send their image to the printer.

Year 1 - Typing

Assessment focus area: Digital Literacy & Information Technology

Beginning (**Must**)	Developing (**Should**)	Mastering (**Could**)
Log into Purple Mash.	Type using both hands. Follow the good posture advice whilst sitting at the computer.	Place fingers in the correct position on the keyboard.

Lesson 1: Use one of the typing apps on the iPads
Lesson 2 & 3: Complete 2Type activities on Purple Mash
Lesson 4: Use the home row keys
Lesson 5 & 6: Use 2Publish on Purple Mash

Lesson 1
Use one of the typing apps on the iPads

Introduction
Explain that when we use computers we have to be good at typing in order to use computers quickly.

Introduce the children to typing on the iPads using the Bee Typing and Class Typing apps, explaining how to use the apps.

Activity
Children use one of the iPad apps, Bee Typing or Typing Class.

Plenary

Create a competition to see who can type words fasters - ask for volunteers to come to the front to type words that you dictate.

Lesson 2 & 3
Complete 2Type activities on Purple Mash

Introduction
Remind children how to log into Purple Mash, which can be found on the school Intranet > Students > Purple Mash.

Direct the students to Tools > 2Type. Click on Introduction to Typing, and explain to the children that in order to become faster at typing, they need to place their fingers in the correct starting position.

Then model doing one of the activities, for example, 'Instruction Keys'. Before children begin the activity, just play the 'Good Posture Tips' advice.

Activity
All children should start with the Instruction Keys activity before moving on to one of the other 2Type activities of their choice.

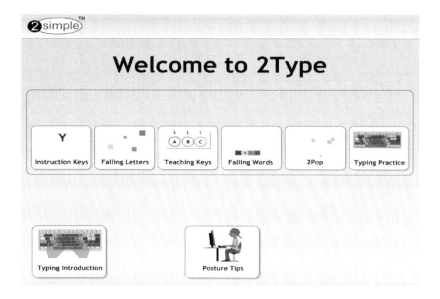

Plenary

Bringing the children back to the carpet, ask for a volunteer to demonstrate doing the Falling Words activity. Who is able to type the words before they fall to the bottom of the screen?

Lesson 4
Use the home row keys

Introduction
Introduce the children to Dance Mat Typing, explaining that in today's lesson they will learn how to type the keys on the home row as well as letters e, i, r and u (http://www.bbc.co.uk/guides/z3c6tfr#zgkpn39).

Activity
Make sure that children are on the website for this activity, and they are wearing the headphones (http://www.bbc.co.uk/guides/z3c6tfr#zgkpn39). They should then begin doing the typing tasks, beginning at Level 1.

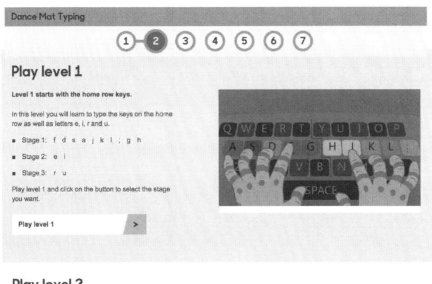

Plenary
Explain that next lesson, children will use their typing skills to begin word processing. Bringing the children to the carpet, ask for volunteers to come forward to write a word that you dictate as quickly as they can into Word. Set the font size to 60 beforehand, so that everyone can see the words being typed.

Lesson 5 & 6
Use 2Publish on Purple Mash

Introduction
Using Purple Mash, model for the children how to access 2Publish (Tools > 2Publish). Explain that in today's lesson, children will draw two pictures and then add a sentence underneath each one to describe a topic of their choice (or a topic that you give them). Begin by clicking on the 'All About' template - demonstrate drawing a picture and writing a sentence.

Activity
Children should open up 2Publish on Purple Mash, and following your instructions, drawing two pictures, writing a sentence for each one. When they have finished, and you have checked, they can print their work.

As an extension or for the following lesson, children can use one of the other 2Publish templates in order to practise their typing skills.

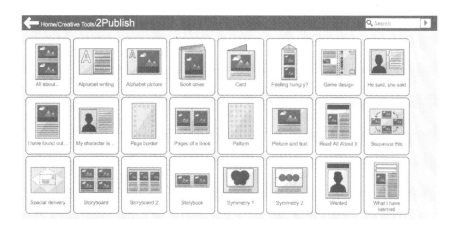

Plenary

Once children have printed and saved their work, choose volunteers to present what they have done to the rest of the class.

Year 1 - Programmable Toys

Assessment focus area: Digital Literacy & Information Technology

Beginning (**Must**)	Developing (**Should**)	Mastering (**Could**)
Log into Purple Mash.	Make several different drawings, using a range of tools.	Send work to the printer. Save and retrieve work.

Lesson 1 & 2: Program Scratch on the iPads
Lesson 3: Program virtual Bee-Bots
Lesson 4 & 5: Program physical Bee-Bots
Lesson 6: Create a game using 2DIY 3D
Lesson 7: Control Dash using the iPad app, Go
Lesson 8: Create paths for Dash to follow
Lesson 9 & 10: Create music on the xylophone using Dash

Lesson 1 & 2
Program Scratch on the iPads

Introduction
Explain to the children that programming just means giving a computer instructions to follow. Show children how to use Scratch on the iPads. Demonstrate changing the background image in Scratch, and you can also show how to change the Scratch cat to a different character. When we're ready, we can begin to program our character to perform different moves. Show how this can be done by dragging different blocks of code into the Program window at the bottom.

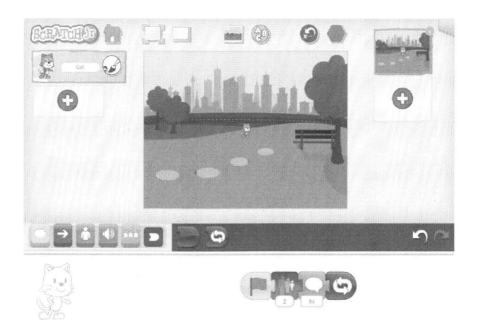

Activity
Children can play with Scratch Jnr, experimenting with different blocks of code to program their character to move on-screen.

Extension Activity:
Give students 10 minutes to try Daisy the Dino in free play mode. Once this time is up, ask children to enter the Challenge mode. Show examples of how to program the Dino to do different moves in sequence. (This requires dragging the instructions from the Commands window into the Program window, and then clicking Play.)

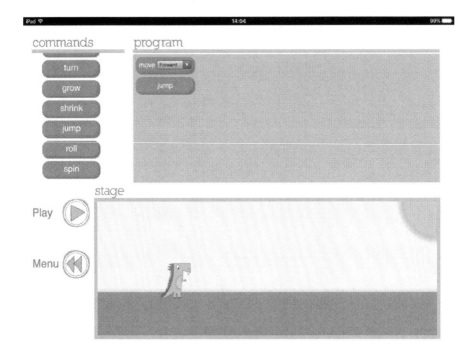

Plenary
Ask for volunteers to demonstrate programming their character to move in different ways on the screen, e.g. to move to the right of the screen and then grow in size.

Lesson 3
Program virtual Bee-Bots

Introduction
In this lesson, students will program virtual Bee-Bots. Demonstrate how to access the Bee-Bot program on the computer and how to display different views. Bring up one of the maps, and ask a volunteer to come forward to program the Bee-Bot to move around the map. Explain that the instructions we give to the Bee-Bot have a special name called "algorithms".

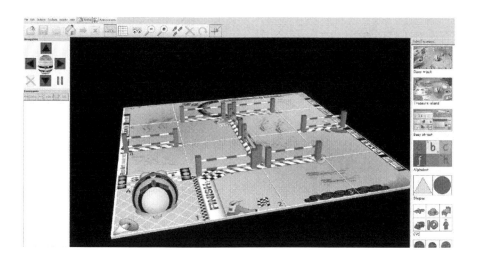

Activity
Students complete the different challenges and practise programming the virtual Bee-Bots to navigate the on-screen map.

Plenary
Ask for volunteers to come up to present what they have learnt. Does anyone remember the name we give to the instructions? Elicit from the children that we have been using algorithms.

Lesson 4 & 5
Program physical Bee-Bots

For these lessons, please make sure that you have booked out the Bee-Bots and Bee-Bot mats.

Introduction
Sit children in a circle, and show them a physical Bee-Bot. Look together at the different buttons on the Bee-Bot, revising how these represent different commands that we can use.

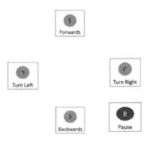

What programming commands can we use?
What do they do?
How can we record them on our whiteboards?

Using a whiteboard, demonstrate using the symbols to draw the commands in order for the Bee-Bot to move in a straight line. Now, ask the students to draw out the commands necessary for the Bee-Bot to move in the shape of a square. Ask for a volunteer to use the commands he or she has written to program the Bee-Bot, checking to see if it will move in the shape of a square.

Activity
Students experiment with Bee-Bots using the Bee-Bot mats.

Extension Activity:
Ask students to write algorithms to instruct the Bee-Bots to
move in the shapes of different numbers, e.g.

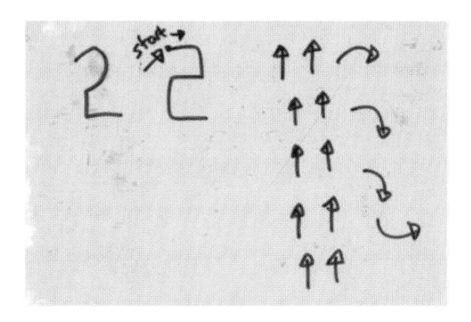

Plenary
Sit children back in a circle. Using one of the Bee-Bot mats,
ask different students to come forward in order to program a
Bee-Bot to move to different locations on the mat.

Lesson 6
Create a game using 2DIY 3D

Introduction

Using the computers in the labs, students create their own maze game. Model how to create a good maze using 2DIY 3D.

Activity

Students create a maze using 2DIY 3D.

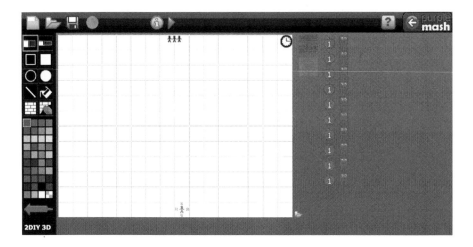

Plenary

Using NetSupport, display students' work, which they have completed.

Lesson 7
Control Dash using the iPad app, Go

For lessons 7 to 10, Dash & Dot kits are required. Ideally, one robot set and iPad should be shared between no more than 4 or 5 children. Make sure that each group is at a good distance apart.

Introduction

Explain that in this lesson children will learn how to control the robot, Dash, using the iPad app, Go. Model opening up Go on the iPad, and then show students how to use the interface to control Dash: make his head move around, move him around, get him to make different sounds and light up. Ask for a volunteer to come forward to see if they can use the controls on the iPad to make Dash blink.

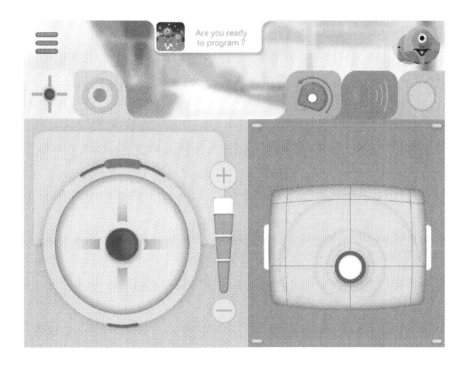

Activity
Students experiment with using the Go app on the iPad to control Dash & Dot.

Plenary
Ask: has anyone worked out how to record their voice on Dash & Dot? Bring forward volunteers to demonstrate using Dash & Dot.

Lesson 8
Create paths for Dash to follow

Introduction

Sitting the children down in a circle, tell them that in this lesson they will learn some basic programming using Dash and Dot. Using the iPad app, Path, children will need to design a path for Dash to follow. Model this on the iPad:

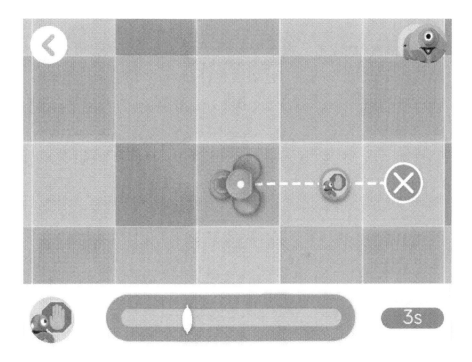

Dash will move along the path as it has been drawn out on the iPad. Explain how we can also add different sounds along this path, which Dash will make in the same sequence as he moves along the path.

Activity
Students use the Path app to draw different paths for Dash to take. As the students advance, they can unlock new themes and special animations.

Plenary
Making sure that children are sat in a circle, ask for a volunteer to program Dash to move along a path within the circle that the children have made.

Lesson 9 & 10
Create music on the xylophone using Dash

Introduction

Explain that in this lesson, the children will be composing music for Dash to play. They will be using the Xylo app on the iPad and the xylophone accessory.

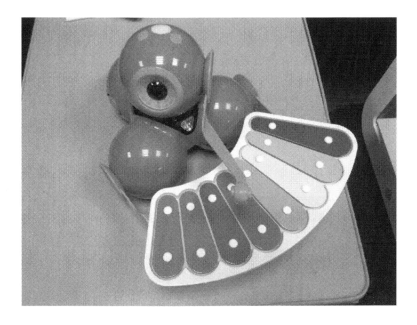

First, model how to attach the xylophone accessory to Dash's body. Then, ask: what do we need to connect next? Elicit that the next thing we need to attach is the mallet, which should connect to the left side of Dash's head. Once these two parts are attached, open up the Xylo app:

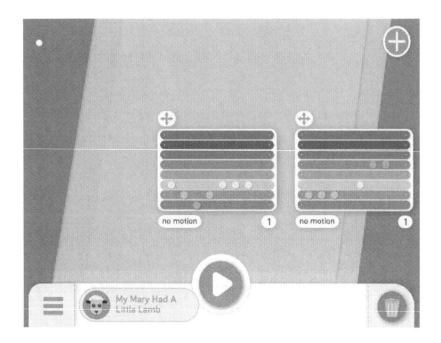

Show the children how, by tapping on the different colours, we can create a sequence of different sounds, as each colour represents a different note. You can demonstrate this by playing one of the readymade tunes, e.g. My Mary Had A Little Lamb.

Activity
The children experiment with composing their own music using the Xylo app and Dash.

Plenary
Ask for volunteers to play the music that they have composed using the Xylo app.

Year 1 - Create a Story

Assessment focus area: Digital Literacy & Information Technology

Beginning (**Must**)	Developing (**Should**)	Mastering (**Could**)
Log into Purple Mash.	Complete Simple City tasks. Create a simple animation using Toontastic and 2Animate. Write a short story using 2Create a Story, which includes at least three pages.	Send work to the printer. Add sound to animation on 2Animate. Save and retrieve work.

Lesson 1: Complete challenges in Simple City
Lesson 2 & 3: Create a story using Toontastic (iPad lessons)
Lesson 4 & 5: Create an animation using 2Animate
Lesson 6 & 7: Make a simple story using 2Create a Story on Purple Mash

Lesson 1
Complete challenges in Simple City

Introduction
Show students how to open up Simple City from Purple Mash
(Tools > Simple City).

From the home page of Simple City, explain that Simple City
represents a city where people live. The city has different
services and attractions. Explore an example with the
students, e.g. the hospital, and show one of the videos.

Activity
Students explore Simple City, and they should complete the
Question challenges.

Plenary

Open up one of the places in Simple City and select the Questions option. Invite volunteers to answer the questions.

Lesson 2 & 3
Create a story using Toontastic (iPad lessons)

Introduction
In this lesson, students will be creating their own animation using the iPad app, Toontastic. Model how to use the app by following these steps:

1. When opening Toontastic, students should click 'Create Cartoon'.

2. Remind students that stories have different stages, a beginning, middle and end. Students click on 'Setup', which will be the beginning of their story.

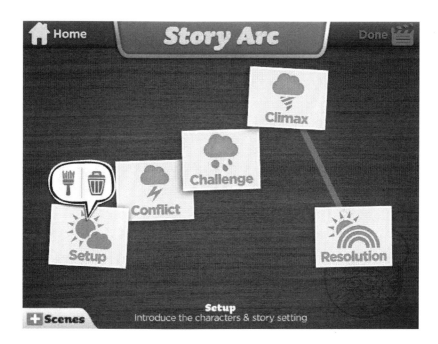

3. The next step is for students to choose a setting.

4. With the setting selected, explain to students that they will need to choose their characters. When they are happy with the setting and characters, students can click the 'Start' button. Explain that everything they say after this point will be recorded. Model creating an example animation in which you move the character on the screen whilst recording a voiceover.

Activity
Students create at least one animation. After creating an animation, students should add music and click 'Done' when finished.

To save and publish students' work, the animations can be exported to the iPad's Camera Roll and uploaded to your Google Drive.

Plenary

Showcase examples of students' work using one of the iPad's or a projector. Discuss what works well in each animation and what could be improved.

Lesson 4 & 5
Create an animation using 2Animate

Introduction

Explain that over the next two lessons students will be creating an animation using a Purple Mash program called 2Animate. Model how to access 2Animate (from the Purple Mash homepage > Tools > 2Animate).

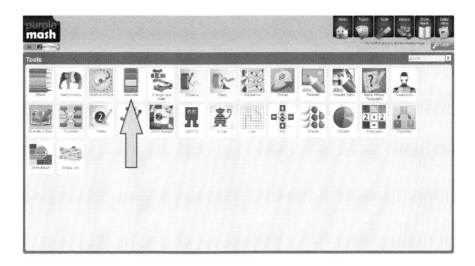

Demonstrate how to use 2Animate by creating one slide at a time. Show the students that, in order to save time, they can duplicate slides by dragging the image along the timeline. By doing this, the image can be changed a little each time in order to create the animation.

Activity

Students go ahead and create an animation about force using 2Animate. Every student's animation should include a background image and last for at least 20 seconds. At the end of each lesson, students can save their work.

Plenary

Share students' animations using NetSupport. Discuss as a class what students like about each animation, and what could be improved.

Lesson 6 & 7
Make a simple story using 2Create a Story on Purple Mash

Introduction
Show students how to open up 2Create a Story from Purple Mash (Tools > 2Create a Story). Click on 'My simple story'.

Model how to begin by creating a picture, and then adding text underneath.

Once upon a time there was a farmer working on his land.

Explain to students that their story should include at least three pages: a beginning, middle and end.

Plenary

Using NetSupport, review students' work. Invite volunteers to read their stories to the rest of the class. Students should have saved their work.

Year 1 - Finding Images

Assessment focus area: Digital Literacy & Information Technology

Beginning (**Must**)	Developing (**Should**)	Mastering (**Could**)
Log into Purple Mash.	Complete work that can be printed. Use the keyboard to type simple words.	Send work to the printer. Save and retrieve work.

Lesson 1: Paint an image of fireworks
Lesson 2: Create a greetings card
Lesson 3 & 4: Create a slideshow presentation
Lesson 5: Create a poster about firework safety

Lesson 1
Paint an image of fireworks

Introduction
Explain to students that many types of big celebrations have something called fireworks. Ask: does anyone know what fireworks are? Fireworks are explosions that are used to create a colourful display in the night sky.

Show students part of this video of the fireworks in London, which were used to celebrate the new year of 2016:
https://www.youtube.com/watch?v=bmZ2bpJKXUI

In this lesson, students will be creating their own firework display using a paint program in Purple Mash. Demonstrate for students how to access and log into Purple Mash. Then Tools > Paint Projects > Fireworks. Model how to use the application, selecting different pen colours and pen thickness.

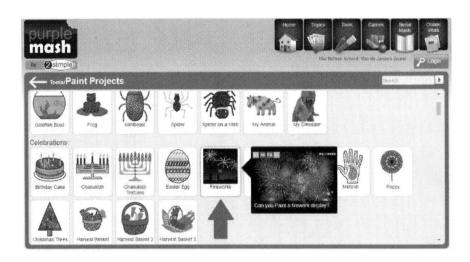

Activity

Students go ahead to create their firework display. Once finished, they should type their name at the bottom of their work and save.

Plenary

Print some selected examples of students' displays.
Encourage these students to share their work with the rest of the class.

Lesson 2
Create a greetings card

Introduction

Ask students what they normally receive for their birthday or Christmas. Elicit that it is common to send greeting cards for birthday and Christmas. In this lesson, students will be designing their own greeting card.

Remind students how to access and log into Purple Mash. Then demonstrate how to access the greeting card template (Tools > 2Publish Plus > Blank Greeting Card).

Show students how to insert text by clicking on the "Write Message Here" section. Model how to change the text size, colour and font. Point out that it is also possible to create a border for the card by clicking inside the image of a magnifying glass and creating a design.

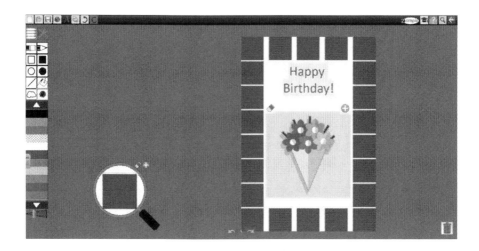

Activity

Students create their perfect greetings card. They should complete each of the three sections of the card. When they are finished, show them how to send their work to the printer.

Plenary

Invite volunteers to present their card to the rest of the class. What do the other students like about the cards created?

Lesson 3 & 4
Create a slideshow presentation

Introduction

Begin the lesson by brainstorming with the students all of the different types of celebrations that they can think of. As students contribute their ideas, write these down on the whiteboard. In this lesson, students will be creating a slideshow of images for each type of celebration using the blank slide show template (Tools > 2Publish Plus > Blank slide show).

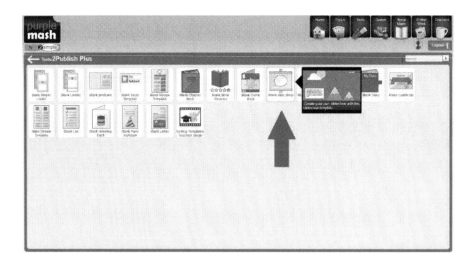

Model for the students how to insert clip art, speech bubbles and text. Explain that if the clip art that the students want is not available, they should use the drawing tools within the program to create their own designs.

Activity

Students should create at least two slides (clicking the "Add Page" icon each time they want to add a new page).

Plenary

Using NetSupport again, display the best work that you have seen. Discuss with the class why this work is particularly good - e.g. use of text, clip art, creative drawings, etc.

Lesson 5
Create a poster about firework safety

Introduction
Remind students about how many events are celebrated with fireworks. Ask: are there any dangers with fireworks? Elicit that although fireworks produce impressive displays, it is important that we know how to be safe around fireworks.

Show students this video about firework safety:
https://www.youtube.com/watch?v=WuaXp4wXnyo

Explain to students that in this lesson we will be creating a poster about firework safety. Model how to access the Firework Safety Poster template, this time by typing "fireworks" into the search bar. Click on the Fireworks Safety Poster template. Model how to drag in pictures and resize on the template. Then ask students to contribute their ideas for how we can keep safe around fireworks, which can be typed up onto the template.

2. Select "Firework Safety Poster".

1. Type the word "fireworks" into the search bar.

Activity

Students complete the Firework Safety Poster template, adding images and text. The poster should include at least two rules for how to keep safe with fireworks and then saved.

Plenary

Print out the best posters for display. Invite students to show their displays to the rest of the class and share what they have learnt.

Year 2 - Digital Citizenship

Assessment focus area: Digital Literacy & Information Technology

Beginning (**Must**)	Developing (**Should**)	Mastering (**Could**)
Log into Purple Mash. Identify one way we can keep safe when using the Internet.	Provide examples of things we can do with the Internet. Identify at least two ways we can keep safe when using the Internet. Make several different designs, using a range of tools.	Identify three or more ways we can keep safe when using the Internet. Cite examples of which personal information should be kept private online (e.g. name, address and school). Save and retrieve work.

Lesson 1: Talk about how we use the Internet
Lesson 2: Use Mashcams tool to create a character display with top tips for using the Internet
Lesson 3: Keep your personal information private

Lesson 1
Talk about how we use the Internet

Introduction
Ask the children what they know about the Internet. Elicit that the Internet is what connects computers to one another, so that we can communicate and share information.

Then watch this video (https://www.youtube.com/watch?v=vUO7t92k4Xg) that shows how 7-year-old Jeremiah uses the Internet. Stop the video at 2 minutes 28 seconds and recap on the main uses of the Internet, e.g:

- Send email messages, which take just 1 or 2 seconds to arrive
- Buy things from shops on the other side of the world
- Talk to friends when it is not possible to meet up

For the main activity children will be using Purple Mash. Demonstrate how to log into Purple Mash, which can be found on the school Intranet > Students > Purple Mash (https://www.purplemash.com/sch/bsrdj). Explain to the children that they will use their login badge, which you will hand out once they are ready to go to the computers.

Activity
Children should click Tools > 2Paint. They should use the different brush tools and colours to draw a picture of themselves using the computer. When finished, model how to save the image (as shown below). As an extension, the children may design a background for their image and type some ways the Internet can be used.

Plenary

Make sure all the children save their work. Using NetSupport, share examples of children's work with the rest of the class.

Lesson 2
Use Mashcams tool to create a character display with top tips for using the Internet

Introduction
Watch the video of Jeremiah again with the children (which can be found at https://www.youtube.com/watch?v=vUO7t92k4Xg. What were the top three tips that Jeremiah gave about using the computer?

Elicit from the children the following:

1. Always ask your parents (or a teacher) first
2. Only talk to people you know
3. Stick to places that are just right for you

Then introduce children to the Mashcam tool on Purple Mash (Tools > Mashcam). Show them how to take a photo of themselves using the webcam (students will need to click on the icon of a camera).

Activity
Students log onto Purple Mash and click on Mashcam. Using this tool, students should choose a character and then take a photo of themselves using the webcam. Once this has been done, they should write at least one tip in the speech bubble about how to use the Internet.

As an extension, students can record a message about themselves using the record button.

Plenary

Children can save and print their work once they have finished.

Lesson 3
Keep your personal information private

Introduction

Explain that we are going to watch a video about two children called Lee and Kim:
https://www.youtube.com/watch?v=NxYily6t4LQ

After you have shown this video, ask the children: what is personal information? Elicit that personal information is private and should not be given to strangers - for example, your name, address and school.

Invite answers from the children about what they would do if someone they didn't know asked for their name and address. Discuss what information we should keep private, and then model for the children how to create a spider diagram of some different examples of private information using 2Connect on Purple Mash.

Activity
Children should access 2Connect on Purple Mash:

Children should write at least three examples of personal (private) information on their spider diagram. As an extension, they can add images.

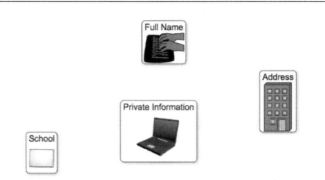

Plenary

Review with the children their understanding of personal information. Check that everyone knows personal information is what makes us unique and is the important information that can be used to identify us. Because this information is so special, we should be careful who we share it with when we meet people (offline and online).

Year 2 - Design

Assessment focus area: Digital Literacy & Information Technology

Beginning (**Must**)	Developing (**Should**)	Mastering (**Could**)
Log into Purple Mash.	Make several different designs, using a range of tools.	Save and retrieve work.

Lesson 1: Create a picture of a bear
Lesson 2: Design a 3D model car
Lesson 3: Create a design using Paint Projects in Purple Mash
Lesson 4: Create an animation using 2animate
Lesson 5: Design a 3D Maze

Lesson 1
Create a picture of a bear

Introduction

Demonstrate for the children how to log into Purple Mash, which can be found on the school Intranet > Students > Purple Mash (https://www.purplemash.com/sch/bsrdj). Explain to the children that they will use their login badge, which you will hand out once they are ready to go off to the computers.

Model clicking Tools > 2Paint. You can show the video tutorial (look at the video icon on the top right-hand side). Demonstrate using the different brush tools and colours to draw a picture of yourself. When finished, model how to save the image (as shown below).

Activity
Using their login badges, children go ahead and access 2Paint. They should draw a picture of themselves using the different paint tools available. As an extension, the children should design a background for their image.

Plenary
Make sure all the children save their work. Using NetSupport, share examples of children's work with the rest of the class.

Lesson 2
Design a 3D model car

Introduction

Explain that today children will be designing a 3D model car - when the children finish their design, they will be able to print it out and build it!

Remind children how to access Purple Mash. Then show them how to access the 2Design & Make app shown below (from Purple Mash, click on Tools and then 2Design & Make):

Model how to change the design of the car. If possible, print out an example to show the children how it could look when they begin to cut it out and fold.

Activity

Children log onto Purple Mash and create their designs. When the children have finished, they can print them out and begin cutting and folding them.

Plenary
Share children's model cars with the rest of the class.

Lesson 3
Create a design using Paint Projects

Introduction
Show the children the Paint Projects application on Purple Mash. Explore a few examples with the children. Ask the children to choose one of the paint projects to work on.

Activity
Using Purple Mash, children choose a paint project to develop into their own unique design.

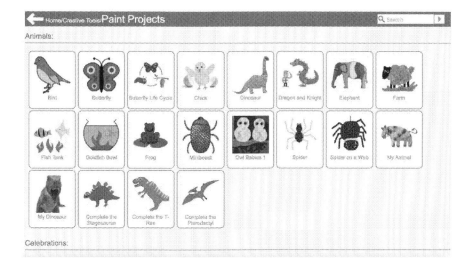

Plenary
Children should save their work.

Lesson 4
Create an animation using 2animate

Introduction
Model how to access 2animate from Purple Mash (Tools > 2Animate). Explain that in today's lesson, children will be creating an animation. Demonstrate how to use this application to create an animation.

Activity
Children create an animation using 2animate.

Plenary
Using NetSupport, share different examples of students' work.

Lesson 5
Design a 3D Maze

Introduction
Ask: what is a maze? Explain that a maze is a confusing path with walls on either side, and the player has to find their way out. In today's lesson, we will be designing our own maze. Model how to access 2DIY 3D (Tools > 2DIY 3D). Show an example of building a maze.

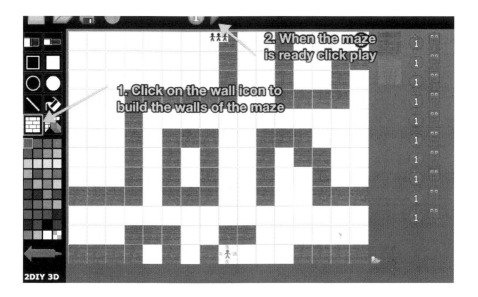

Activity
The children should design their maze to be as interesting as possible, using the full range of tools available.

When children have finished, they can swap over with a partner to have a go at each other's mazes.

Plenary
Using NetSupport, ask for volunteers to present their maze to the rest of the class. Discuss with the class what makes a good maze, referring to the visual elements in the design.

Year 2 – Word Processing

Assessment focus area: Digital Literacy & Information Technology

Beginning (**Must**)	Developing (**Should**)	Mastering (**Could**)
Log into Purple Mash.	Type using both hands. Follow the good posture advice whilst sitting at the computer.	Place fingers in the correct position on the keyboard.

Lesson 1: Play typing game
Lesson 2: Use the home row keys
Lesson 3: Use 2Publish on Purple Mash
Lesson 4: Use 2Publish Extra on Purple Mash
Lesson 5 & 6: Create a storybook using 2Publish storybook template

Lesson 1
Play typing game

Introduction

Remind children how to log into Purple Mash, which can be found on the school Intranet > Students > Purple Mash (https://www.purplemash.com/sch/bsrdj).

Direct the students to Tools > 2Type. Click on Introduction to Typing, and explain to the children that in order to become faster at typing, they need to place their fingers in the correct starting position.

Then model doing one of the activities, for example, 'Instruction Keys'. Before children begin the activity, just play the 'Good Posture Tips' advice.

Activity

All children should start with the Instruction Keys activity before moving on to one of the other 2Type activities of their choice.

Plenary

Bringing the children back to the carpet, ask for a volunteer to demonstrate doing the Falling Words activity. Who is able to type the words before they fall to the bottom of the screen?

Lesson 2
Use the home row keys

Introduction
Introduce the children to Dance Mat Typing
(http://www.bbc.co.uk/guides/z3c6tfr#zgkpn39), explaining that
in today's lesson they will learn how to type the keys on the
home row as well as letters e, i, r and u.

Activity
Make sure that children are on the website
(http://www.bbc.co.uk/guides/z3c6tfr#zgkpn39) for this activity,
and they are wearing the headphones. They should then
begin doing the typing tasks, beginning at Level 1.

Plenary
Explain that next lesson, children will use their typing skills to
begin word processing. Bringing the children to the carpet, ask
for volunteers to come forward to write a word that you dictate
as quickly as they can into Word. Set the font size to 60
beforehand so that everyone can see the words being typed.

Lesson 3
Use 2Publish on Purple Mash

Introduction

Using Purple Mash, model for the children how to access 2Publish (Tools > 2Publish). Explain that in today's lesson, children will draw two pictures and then add a sentence underneath each one to describe a topic of their choice (or a topic that you give them). Begin by clicking on the 'All About' template - demonstrate drawing a picture and writing a sentence.

Activity

Children should open up 2Publish on Purple Mash, and following your instructions, drawing two pictures, writing a sentence for each one. When they have finished, and you have checked, they can print their work.

Plenary

Once children have printed and saved their work, choose volunteers to present what they have done to the rest of the class.

Lesson 4
Use 2Publish Extra on Purple Mash

Introduction
Begin by modelling for the children how to access 2Publish Extra (Tools > 2Publish Extra), and click on the template 'I have found out…' Based on a topic or project you have been doing in class, explain that in today's lesson children will make a display about what they have found out about that topic or project. Demonstrate how to draw and write text.

Activity
Children should open 2Publish Extra on Purple Mash, and following your instructions, create a display based on a project or topic that they have been doing in class. When children have finished, and you have checked, they can print their work.

Plenary
Once children have printed and saved their work, choose volunteers to present what they have done to the rest of the class.

Lesson 5 & 6
Create a storybook using 2Publish storybook template

Introduction
Explain to the children that over the next two lessons, they will be creating a storybook. Demonstrate opening up 2Publish and then clicking on the Storyboard template. Explain that their story must follow a sequence of events with a beginning, middle and end. Model writing a story - one sentence for each scene. Then tell the children that they will need to draw a picture to go with each sentence.

Activity
Children use 2Publish storyboard template to write their story. They should make sure that they save their work and print the story once finished.

Plenary
Children should present their stories to the rest of the class.

Year 2 - Game Testers

Assessment focus area: Computer Science & Digital Literacy

Beginning (**Must**)	Developing (**Should**)	Mastering (**Could**)
Log into Purple Mash.	Save work in Purple Mash for retrieval later. Type using both hands.	Place fingers in the correct position on the keyboard. Create tables, pictograms and block graphs.

Lesson 1: Program Scratch on the iPads
Lesson 2 & 3: Solve problems using the Osmo App
Lesson 4: Complete 2Code Activities
Lesson 5: Complete 2Code Activities

Lesson 1
Program Scratch on the iPads

Introduction

Show children how to use Scratch on the iPads. Explain that this program is similar to Daisy the Dino, just a little more complex. Demonstrate changing the background image in Scratch, and you can also show how to change the Scratch cat to a different character. When we're ready, we can begin to program our character to perform different moves. Show how this can be done by dragging different blocks of code into the Program window at the bottom.

Activity

Children play with Scratch Jnr, experimenting with different blocks of code to program their character to move on-screen.

Plenary

Ask for volunteers to demonstrate programming their character to move in different ways on the screen, e.g. to move to the right of the screen and then grow in size.

Lesson 2 & 3
Solve problems using the Osmo App

Introduction
Begin by introducing the Osmo accessory kit as a way to connect the physical world (what we can touch with our hands) with the digital world (what we see on the screen). Start with Tangram, explaining that this game is an ancient Chinese puzzle. Remind children that we have to be extra careful with the iPads during this activity because we have to remove the protective cases in order to use Osmo.

Activity
Working in twos or threes, children play tangram, recreating the different shapes that they see onscreen.

As an extension or for the follow up lesson, children can have a go at one of the other Osmo apps (Newton, Numbers, Masterpiece or Words).

Plenary
Find out what the children enjoyed most about these activities. What was most challenging?

Lesson 4
Complete 2Code Activities

Introduction

Log into Purple Mash and click on 2Code, and then 'Fun with Fish'. Complete the first two challenges with the students - moving the tuna right and moving the crab left. Demonstrate how to drag commands into the programming window. Explain to students that they need to work through as many of these activities as they can.

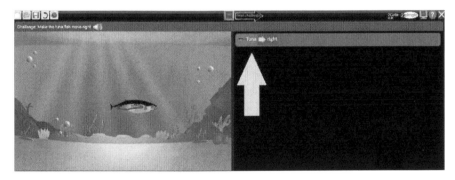

Activity

Students complete the 'Fun with Fish' activities. They can then move onto the other activities, including 'Bubbles' and 'Air Traffic Control'.

Plenary

Invite students to the front to demonstrate how to complete the Air Traffic Control activities.

Lesson 5
Complete 2Code Activities

Introduction

Following the previous lesson, explain to students that they will continue to create games and debug code. Ask: what do you think it means to debug code? Elicit that debugging refers to the process of looking for and correcting mistakes in computer code.

In this lesson students will focus on the 'Superheroes' code activity. Start by demonstrating and inviting volunteers to help get the superhero to fly off the building.

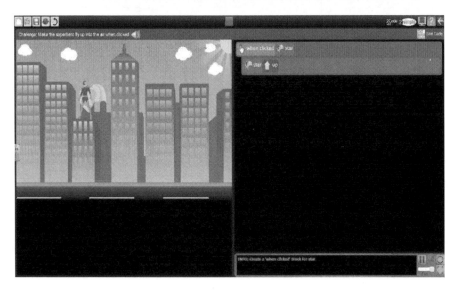

Activity

Students complete the 'Superheroes' activities. They can then move onto the other activities, including 'Bubbles' and 'Air Traffic Control'.

Plenary

Invite students to the front to demonstrate how to complete the Superheroes activities.

Year 2 - Media Magic

Assessment focus area: Computer Science & Digital Literacy

Beginning (**Must**)	Developing (**Should**)	Mastering (**Could**)
Log into Purple Mash.	Type using both hands. Follow the good posture advice whilst sitting at the computer.	Place fingers in the correct position on the keyboard.

Lesson 1: Program virtual Bee-Bots
Lesson 2: Use Bee-Bot app on iPads
Lesson 3: Start Bee-Bot programming
Lesson 4 & 5: Filming using iMovie

Lesson 1
Program virtual Bee-Bots

Introduction
Remind children of the Bee-Bots they have used in Infant 1. In this lesson, students will program virtual Bee-Bots. Demonstrate how to access the Bee-Bot program on the computer and how to display different views. Bring up one of the maps, and ask a volunteer to come forward to program the bee-bot to move around the map.

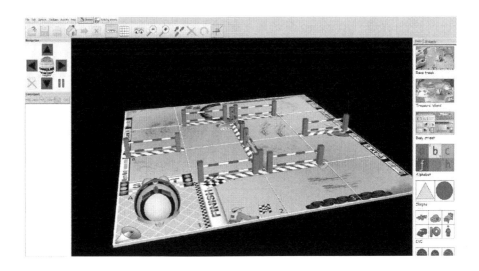

Activity
Students complete the different challenges and practise programming the virtual Bee-Bots to navigate the on-screen map.

Plenary
Ask for volunteers to come up to present what they have learnt.

Lesson 2
Use Bee-Bot app on iPads

Introduction

Ask: what do we call it when we give a computer instructions? Explain that there is a computer inside the Bee-Bots, and we call the instructions "programming". Demonstrate how to open the Bee-Bot app on the iPads and go through a couple of programming challenges with the students.

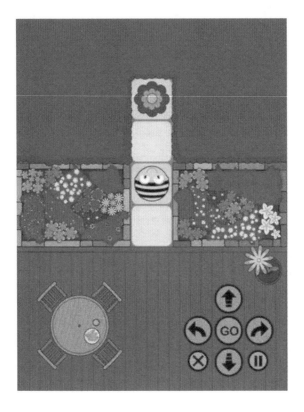

Activity

Students should complete as many of the Bee-Bot challenges as they can.

Plenary
Invite volunteers to demonstrate completing one of the programming challenges.

Lesson 3
Start Bee-Bot programming

Introduction
Gather students in a circle on the carpet. In the middle of the circle put a Bee-Bot mat and Bee-Bot. Show students how to program the Bee-Bot to move along the grid on the mat.

Activity
Children play with the Bee-Bots, programming the bee-bots to navigate different mats.

Plenary
Ask for volunteers to demonstrate programming their Bee-Bot to move in different ways on the mat, e.g. to move to a particular location.

Lesson 4 & 5
Filming using iMovie

Introduction
Provide students with an overview of how to use iMovie on the iPads. Divide the children into groups of threes. At least one child from each group should be responsible for filming on the iPad. This video footage is best filmed using iMovie itself for easy editing.

Activity
In their groups, children film the Bee-Bots. As an extension, they can work together to make an iMovie trailer.

Plenary
Show examples of students' videos to the rest of the class. Discuss what worked well and what could be improved.

Year 3 - Digital Citizenship

Assessment focus area: Digital Literacy

Beginning (**Must**)	Developing (**Should**)	Mastering (**Could**)
Create a basic Word document. Understand what personal information is and what a stranger is. Recognise that not everything on the Internet is true.	Be able to save work and retrieve later. Write sentences in Word, explaining what personal information is and what a stranger is. Use alternative search engines to Google, which are child-friendly.	Write a list using bullet points. Recite the five SMART rules for using the Internet.

Lesson 1: Be kind to others online
Lesson 2: Recognise some dangers of using the Internet
Lesson 3: Know that not everything on the Internet is true
Lesson 4: Remember the SMART rules for using the Internet

Lesson 1
Be kind to others online

Introduction
Make sure that children are sitting on the floor in front of the whiteboard. Read this story about Digiduck:
http://www.kidsmart.org.uk/teachers/ks1/sourcesDuck/projet/DigiDuck-eBook.pdf

Ask: how can you be a good friend on the Internet? Explain to children that they will be making a poster using Microsoft Word. Model how to make use of Word Art and different font styles.

Activity
Using Microsoft Word, children should create a poster with the title: How to be a good friend on the Internet. Children should make use of Word Art and different font styles. Direct children how to save the work in their Pupil Work Space.

Plenary
If children have finished their posters, they should save and print them.

Lesson 2
Recognise some dangers of using the Internet

Introduction
Show children this video about Lee & Kim's Adventure:
https://www.youtube.com/watch?v=-nMUbHuffO8

Ask: what were the top tips for Internet Safety?

After the video, ask: What is a stranger?
> •A stranger is someone you do not know.
> •Recap stranger danger in the real world.
> •Lee and Kim were promised 'treasure' if they followed the 'bear', but sometimes 'strangers' promise things that are not true, to get you to do something you do not want to do.

Ask: what is personal information?
> •Personal information is the details about you that only people you know or trust should know.

Activity
Using Microsoft Word, children should complete these two sentences:
1. A stranger is someone who…
2. Personal information is…

Remind children to experiment with different font sizes and styles. If any children complete these two sentences, ask them to write a list of any examples of personal information. When they completed this task, they can save and print their work.

Plenary
Review children's answers. What are some examples of personal information? Then remind children of SID's top tips from the video.

Lesson 3
Know that not everything on the Internet is true

Introduction
Show the children the spoof website Tomato Spider:
http://webfronter.com/rbkc/tomatospider/

Explain that you are quite excited about it because you would never have believed it was true unless it was on the Internet! Children to have a look at the website in more detail jotting down anything that surprises them! Bring the children back together and explain that actually it is a made-up website - none of the information on here is true. Remind children of last lesson, discussing the fact that sometimes people are not who they say they are.

Activity
Ask: when you use the Internet, what search engines do you normally use? Introduce the children to these child-friendly search engines:
www.kiddle.co
www.kidsclick.org
www.kidrex.org/
Children should look for information about rainforests (or a topic of your choice) using these search engines. Using a pencil and paper, ask the children to note down some interesting facts they learn from their research about the rainforest, reminding them to also note down the name of the website where they got the information.

Plenary
What did children learn from their research? Ask: why is it better for them to use one of these search engines to find out information rather than a search engine like Google? Elicit that these child-friendly search engines provide information that is easier to read.

Lesson 4
Remember the SMART rules for using the Internet

Introduction
Show children this Dongle Stay Safe Video:
https://www.youtube.com/watch?v=VcM7sV9ZrGM

At the end of each question, ask children to share their ideas. Then continue playing the video to show children the explanation. Model how to make a display based on these five letters (S - M - A - R - T) using Word.

Activity
Children make their own display in Word based on the five letters:

S - Safe - Always keep your personal information private.
M - Meeting - Meeting up with a web pal can be dangerous.
A - Accepting - emails from people you don´t know can contain viruses.
R - Reliable - someone online may not be who they say they are.
T - Tell your parent or an adult if something makes you feel uncomfortable or worried.

Plenary
Review children's displays - print the best ones for display.

Year 3 – Communication & E-Safety

Assessment focus area: Digital Literacy

Beginning (**Must**)	Developing (**Should**)	Mastering (**Could**)
Recall SMART rules for using the Internet.	Create a poster using Google Slides. Demonstrate an understanding about how to keep personal information private. Contribute to discussion about safer Internet use.	Articulate the purpose of using avatars online.

Lesson 1 & 2: Be careful when opening emails from strangers
Lesson 3: Access Google Drive to create a Google Drawing
Lesson 4: Access and respond to an email
Lesson 5 & 6: Work collaboratively on a Google Slide

Lesson 1 & 2
Be careful when opening emails from strangers

Introduction
Begin by showing children this video about the SMART rules of the Internet:
https://www.youtube.com/watch?v=VcM7sV9ZrGM

In today's lesson, we will focus on what can happen if you open up emails from people you don't know. Then show children this video of What Should You Accept?
http://www.childnet.com/resources/the-adventures-of-kara-winston-and-the-smart-crew

Activity
Using this poster as an example, ask children to design a better-looking poster using Google Slides:
http://www.kidsmart.org.uk/downloads/create-a-poster.pdf

Plenary
Check that children can explain the poster they have created.

Lesson 3
Access Google Drive to create a Google Drawing

Introduction
Explain to the children that the school uses Google Apps for Education. This is a range of applications created by Google, an American Technology Company. Today we will look at using Google Drawing, which the students will be able to access from their Gmail account. Demonstrate logging into one of the student accounts. Go to gmail.com and type in one of the student usernames. Explain that the first-time students login they will be prompted to change this password.

Note to teacher: At this age, it is recommended for the teacher to keep a copy of all the students' passwords because there will be students who forget.

Once logged in, show the children how to access the Google Drive and create a new Google Drawing. Here is an example:

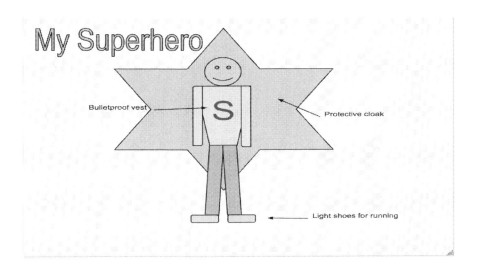

Activity
Students should go ahead and create a Google Drawing. More able learners can label their drawing using arrows and text function.

Plenary
Explain to students that they don't need to save their work in Google Docs, as their work is automatically saved as they type. Ask some students to read aloud their work to the rest of the class.

Lesson 4
Access and respond to an email

Introduction

Ask: what is the most common way of communicating over the Internet? Elicit from the students that email is the most popular form of communication using the Internet. It began just over 20 years ago, and it's a way of sending digital messages really quickly. Demonstrate opening up your Gmail to write a message to the class (to save time, have this in your drafts folder ready to send), e.g.:

Dear Class 1A,

In today's lesson, we will be looking at how to use email. I would like you to read these questions I have written for you below. Please write answers to these questions and respond to me by email.

1. If you could be famous, what would you be famous for?
2. Where is your favourite place in the world?
3. What is the best gift you have ever been given? Why was it so special?
4. Please can you attach your work from last lesson into your email?

I look forward to receiving your responses!

Best wishes,

Your teacher

Then, model for the students how to reply to the message - in an appropriate style:

Dear Mr/Mrs…,

Thanks for your email. Please find my answers to your questions below:

If I could be famous, I would like to be famous for (   )

Etc.

Demonstrate for the students how to attach their work from last lesson into their email by clicking on the Google Drive icon.

Activity
Students should compose and send their email to you.

Plenary
Review some of the emails sent to you, reading some of the children's responses. Did everyone show good manners when communicating online? Discuss that we call good manners online, netiquette. If time, show students the video made by Mr Will at his old school about netiquette:
https://www.youtube.com/watch?v=NYJydonwb3A

Lesson 5 & 6
Work collaboratively on a Google Slide

Introduction
Explain that over the next two lessons the children will be working on a class presentation about rainforests. To do this, we will be using Google Slides, which is an application we use to make presentations. (Create a Google Slide beforehand and share it with the class, making sure they can edit. Include this link (http://kids.mongabay.com) on the first slide for child-friendly information about rainforests). Demonstrate how to write a title on the slide and insert a picture. On each slide the children create, they should type one fact they find out about rainforests.

Tell the children that they will need to go into their email in order to access the Google Slide. Make sure that the students understand that when they access the Google Slide, they will see each other online. **Remind them to be sensible and not make changes on a slide that another child is working on!**

Activity
Children go into their email and access the Google Slide that you have shared with them. They should try to create at least three slides each, include a title, picture and fact on every slide.

Plenary
Display the class Google Slide for everyone to see. What did the children learn about rainforests? How could we improve the appearance of the presentation?

Year 3 - Video Production

Assessment focus area: Digital Literacy & Information Technology

Beginning (**Must**)	Developing (**Should**)	Mastering (**Could**)
Log into Purple Mash. Save work for retrieval next time.	Populate a template with images and text. Create an animation with background images and sound.	Upload animation to Google Drive without support.

Lesson 1 & 2: Create an animation about forces
Lesson 3: Create an animation using ABCYa and upload to the Google Drive
Lesson 4: Select images and write captions (Part 1)
Lesson 5: Select images and write captions (Part 2)
Lesson 6: Create a concept map

Lesson 1 & 2
Create an animation about forces

Introduction

Explain that over the next two lessons students will be creating an animation about at least one type of force using a Purple Mash program called 2Animate. Model how to access 2Animate (from the Purple Mash homepage > Tools > 2Animate).

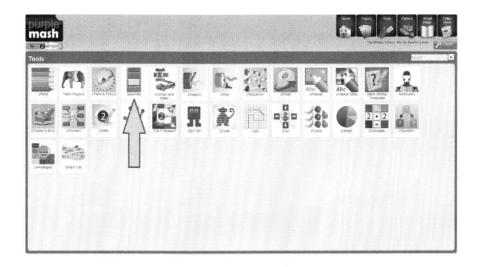

Demonstrate how to use 2Animate by creating one slide at a time. Show the students that, in order to save time, they can duplicate slides by dragging the image along the timeline. By doing this, the image can be changed a little each time in order to create the animation.

Activity

Students go ahead and create an animation about force using 2Animate. Every student's animation should include a background image, sound and last for at least 30 seconds. At the end of each lesson, students should save their work.

Plenary

Share students' animations using NetSupport. Discuss as a class what students like about each animation, and what could be improved.

Lesson 3
Create an animation using ABCYa and upload to the Google Drive

Introduction
Demonstrate using ABCYa
(http://www.abcya.com/animate.htm) to create a short animation. Click Go > Model how to add a background, insert characters and duplicate slides.

Activity
Students should go ahead and create their animation using ABCYa.

For the second part of the lesson, demonstrate how to export the animation by clicking on Export as GIF:

Once the animation has finished exporting, click on Save. Then show the students how to upload this animation to their Google Drive and share with you.

Plenary

Using NetSupport, showcase a student's work on the display. Which animation software did students prefer using, 2Animate or ABCYa?

Lesson 4
Select images and write captions (Part 1)

Introduction

Explain to students that each one of them now has a Purple Mash login card. This means that students will be able to access Purple Mash from home and save their work.

For this lesson, students will be explaining different forces in action. From the Purple Mash home page, click on Topics and then Forces.

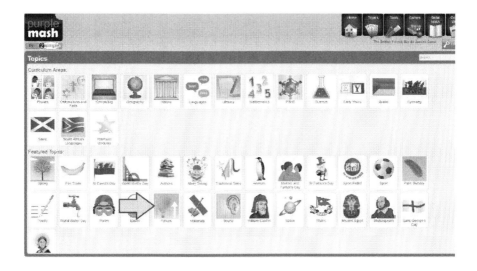

They should then click on the Forces in Action icon. Model how to insert images onto this template by clicking on the green icon with a plus (+) sign. Elicit from the students that the text underneath the image is called a caption.

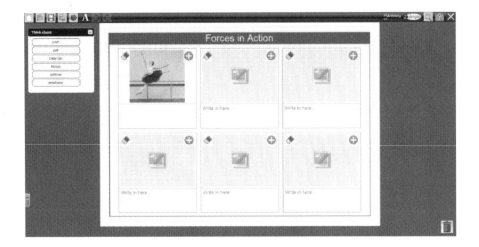

Activity

Students log into Purple Mash using their login badge. They should then go to the Forces topic section, click on the Forces in Action icon and create their own information sheet about forces in action. Once they have finished, students should save and print their work. As an extension, students can complete the Forces in Action v2 activity from this section.

Plenary

Review some examples of the children's designs. What worked well? Did everyone manage to save their work?

Lesson 5
Select images and write captions (Part 2)

Introduction
Recap with the students how to log into Purple Mash. Explain that today students will complete the writing project, Forces v3. Remind students where to find the Forces section (from the Purple Mash home page > Tools > Forces).

Ask for a volunteer to come to the front to insert an image onto the template. Ask the class: what forces are in action here? Discuss a couple more examples.

Activity
Students complete Forces v3 activity. As an extension, students can also complete the Forces 1 activity in which they have to describe how forces are applied. Students should then save and print their work on completion.

Plenary
Ask for volunteers to present their work to the rest of the class.

Lesson 6
Create a concept map

Introduction

Explain to the students that during this lesson they will create something called a concept map to showcase everything they have learnt about forces. Model how to access the concept mapping tool from Purple Mash.

Model how to create the concept map, starting with a blank template. Show the students how each concept should branch out. For example, we can connect the main word in the middle, *Forces* with all the different types of forces, and then each one of these forces should branch out to provide different examples of forces.

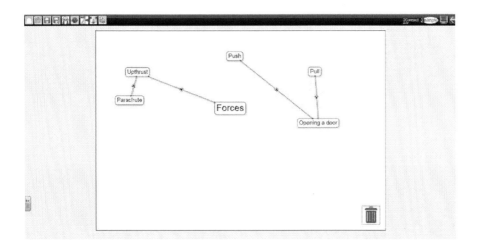

Activity

Students create a concept map. As an extension, they should select the text icon and write down in complete sentences what they understand by each force, using the concept map to help them.

Plenary

Students should print their work for display. Use NetSupport to present students' concept maps on the board, asking for volunteers to present and explain their ideas to the rest of the class.

Year 3 - Programming an Animation

Assessment focus area: Computer Science & Information Technology

Beginning (**Must**)	Developing (**Should**)	Mastering (**Could**)
Plan an animation by creating a storyboard. Choose or select the background for an animation in Scratch.	Create sprites using the Paint tool in Scratch. Put Scratch blocks in the right order.	Use the if/then/else block correctly. Debug (correct mistakes) in the animation. Predict what will happen in a game by looking at the code.

Lesson 1 & 2: Complete 2Code Activities
Lesson 3: Create a storyboard
Lesson 4: Create a character and background
Lesson 5: Start to animate the characters
Lesson 6: Improve the animations

Lesson 1 & 2
Complete 2Code Activities

Introduction

Explain to the students that we will begin by completing some programming activities. Model opening up 2Code from the Purple Mash homepage (Tools > 2Code). For the first activity, go to Fun with Fish program.

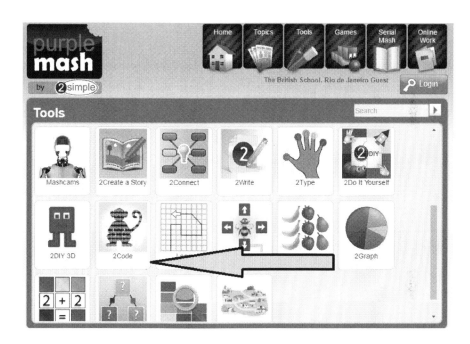

Complete the first two challenges with the students - moving the tuna right and moving the crab left. Demonstrate how to drag commands into the programming window. Ask for different volunteers to come forward to complete the different programming challenges. Explain to students that they need to work through as many of these activities as they can.

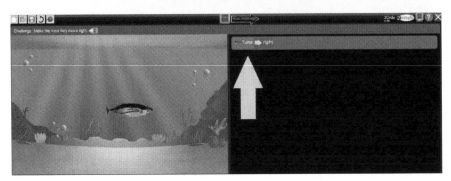

Activity

Students should log into Purple Mash, and complete activities of their choice from 2Code.

Plenary

Review students' understanding of programming. Elicit from students that programming is the process of giving a computer instructions to perform different tasks.

Lesson 3
Create a storyboard

Introduction

Explain to the children that they will be making their own animation using a program called Scratch. Begin by showing them an example animation below:
https://scratch.mit.edu/projects/77278008/ (click on green flag to play the animation).

Before students start to make their animation, they will need to create a storyboard to help them plan the animation. Demonstrate opening the application in Purple Mash called 'Storyboard' (you can search for this in the search bar).

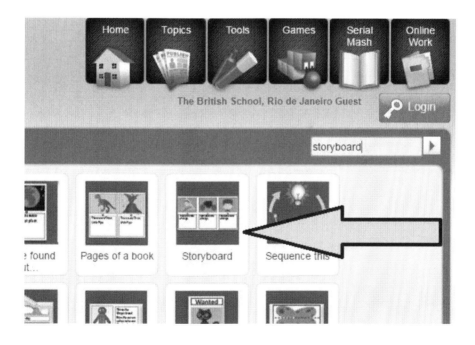

Activity
Once students have logged in and opened up Storyboard from Purple Mash, they should complete the template with drawings and notes about what will happen in their animation.

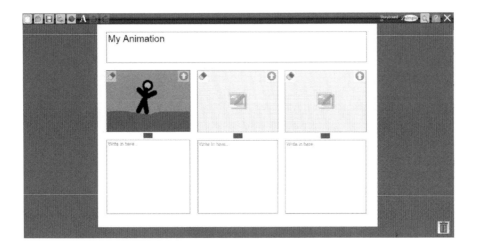

Plenary
Students should save and print their finished work. Ask for volunteers to present their storyboards to the rest of the class. Ask students to identify what they think will make a good animation, e.g. action, music and sound, fun characters, bright colours, etc.

Lesson 4
Create a character and background

Introduction
In this lesson, children will need to create a character and background for their animation. Using Scratch, begin showing children how to create a background using the Paint function in Scratch.

Steps:
1. Once logged in, click on Create.
2. Click on icon of stage and click on tab, Backdrop.

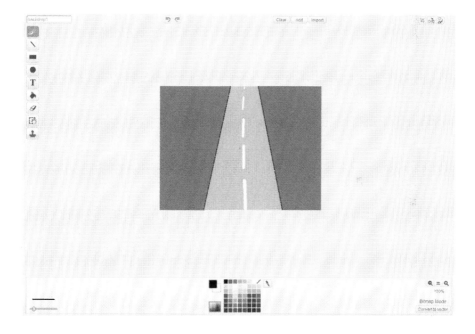

Afterwards, show children how to make their sprite (the character that will be moving on the screen). Children can either paint their own sprite or choose one from the sprite library.

Activity
Children make the background and sprite.

Plenary
Using NetSupport, display best examples of sprites and backgrounds, which children have created.

Lesson 5
Start to animate the characters

Introduction

Explain that the children are now at the point where they will start to program their animations in Scratch, and that this involves converting the storyboard into a program using Scratch blocks.

Show the children how to drag and clip together different programming blocks to start building an animation script. Draw particular attention to the blocks *wait* (in the Control palette), *glide* (in the Motions palette) and *say* (in the Looks palette).

Demonstrate putting this code together below:

Discuss the steps involved in programming and then questions the children should ask themselves if they come across a problem.

Activity
Give the children time to start programming their animations, referring to the storyboard they created in the previous lesson. Encourage the children to solve any problems themselves, without much input from you.

Plenary
Ask the children to share their successes and any challenges they faced. Project some of the animations, discussing how successful they are.

Lesson 6
Improve the animations

Introduction
Demonstrate how to change between different costumes using the *switch costume to* and *next costume* blocks on the Looks palette. For example, you could create a *repeat* block to create the illusion of a sprite walking by repeatedly switching between costumes. You can also show the Sounds tab and how to add different sounds effects.

Activity
Encourage the children to continue to develop their scripts.

Plenary
Ask children to swap their computer with a partner, to get feedback on any improvements that could be made to their Scratch animation.

Year 3 - Music & Sounds

Assessment focus area: Digital Literacy & Information Technology

Beginning (**Must**)	Developing (**Should**)	Mastering (**Could**)
Log into Purple Mash. Save work for retrieval next time.	Populate a template with images and text. Create an animation with background images and sound.	Upload animation to Google Drive without support.

Lesson 1 - Use 2Explore to make a simple piece of music
Lesson 2 - Compose a piece of music using 2Sequence on Purple Mash
Lesson 3 - Create a musical composition using the Isle of Tune website
Lesson 4 - Create a Google Slide with images of objects that make sound
Lesson 5 & 6 - Create music on the xylophone using Dash

Lesson 1
Use 2Explore to make a simple piece of music

Introduction

Show students this video of the Sesame Street song "What I Am" (https://www.youtube.com/watch?v=cyVzjoj96vs). After listening to this music, ask students if they noticed the music repeat in a particular pattern. Explain that we call this a *sequence*. In this lesson, students will be creating their own piece of music, which will require them to create a sequence of different musical notes.

Open up 2Explore from Purple Mash, and explain to students that each image shows a different musical instrument. We can click on any of these instruments in order to make a sound. If the record button is clicked (the red square), then the sequence of music is recorded as the instruments are clicked. The speed of the playback can be changed by dragging the bar (if it is dragged to the right, the music becomes faster). The music made can be repeated by clicking on the loop button. If the new button is clicked, different musical instruments can be selected.

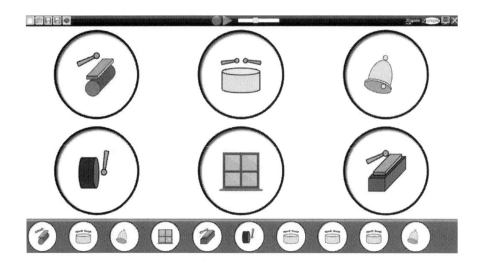

Then open up 2Beat and show the students how the drums can be played at different times by clicking on the squares. As you click on the different squares, explain that what you are doing is programming the computer to play a particular set of sounds. Ask the students what happens to the music when we change the number of beats. Point out that the volume of the individual instruments can also be changed.

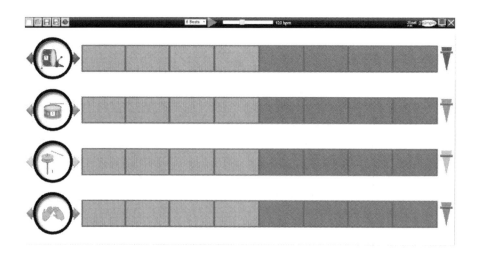

Activity
Students go ahead and explore the different music they can create using 2Explore and 2Beat.

Plenary
Using NetSupport play examples of music that the students have made.

Lesson 2
Compose a piece of music using 2Sequence on Purple Mash

Introduction
Open up 2Sequence from Purple Mash and explain that there are many different sounds here available from different tabs.

Show students the tutorial video that is available on 2Sequence (found on the top right-hand side of the screen). You can also show students this video of the Jurassic Park helicopter landing scene (https://www.youtube.com/watch?v=ghKy8FRhs28) explaining that the students are music directors and will need to create the backing music for the video.

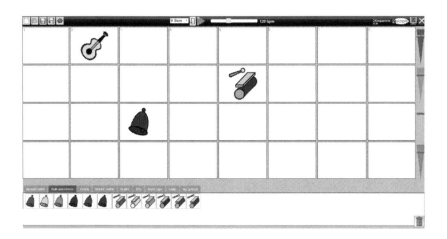

Activity
Ask students to create an appropriate music track to accompany the scene.

Plenary
Invite volunteers to play their scary music. What worked well? What could be improved?

Lesson 3
Create a musical composition using the Isle of Tune website

Introduction
In this lesson, students will be using the Isle of Tune website (isleoftune.com). Explain that they will be creating musical journeys from street layouts. Roadside elements are the instruments and cars are the players.

Click on View Islands, and explore with the students' other musical journeys that have been created.

Activity
Than ask for volunteers to create their own musical composition using the Isle of Tunes website.

Plenary
Review examples of the students' work. What was particularly effective?

Lesson 4
Create a Google Slide with images of objects that make sound

Introduction
Demonstrate for the students how to create a new Google Slide. Explain to the students that they will be inserting and labelling images of items that make sound. Model how to insert an image (Insert > image), and then type a label. Ask for a volunteer to show the rest of the class how to insert and label an image too.

Activity
Students create a one slide presentation that shows different sound producing items.

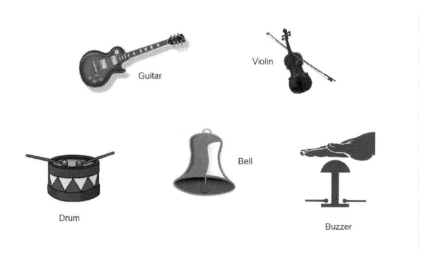

Plenary
Review the examples provided by the students. Print a selection of examples for display.

Lesson 5 & 6
Create music on the xylophone using Dash

Introduction

Explain that in this lesson, the students will be composing music for Dash to play. They will be using the Xylo app on the iPad and the xylophone accessory.

First, model how to attach the xylophone accessory to Dash's body. Then, ask: what do we need to connect next? Elicit that the next thing we need to attach is the mallet, which should connect to the left side of Dash's head. Once these two parts are attached, open up the Xylo app:

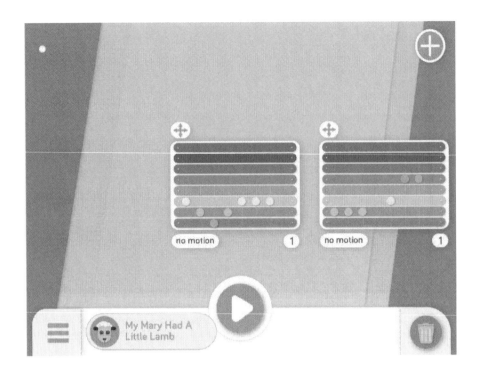

Show the students how, by tapping on the different colours, we can create a sequence of different sounds, as each colour represents a different note. You can demonstrate this by playing one of the readymade tunes, e.g. My Mary Had A Little Lamb.

Activity
The students experiment with composing their own music using the Xylo app and Dash.

Plenary
Ask for volunteers to play the music that they have composed using the Xylo app.

Year 3 - Digital Art

Assessment focus area: Digital Literacy & Information Technology

Beginning (**Must**)	Developing (**Should**)	Mastering (**Could**)
Log into Purple Mash. Save work for retrieval next time. Create a simple drawing using the Wacom pen tablet. Explore information online.	Use three or more different effects from the Wacom pen tablet software, ArtRage Lite.	Recreate an accurate digital representation of a painting using the Wacom pen tablet.

Lesson 1 - Explore the paint projects from Purple Mash
Lesson 2 & 3 - Use a pen tablet to create digital art
Lesson 4 - Explore an online encyclopaedia
Lesson 5 - Research Brazilian artists
Lesson 6 - Recreate chosen artwork using the Wacom pen

Lesson 1
Explore the paint projects from Purple Mash

Introduction
To link with our IPC unit, 'Paintings, Pictures & Photographs' show the students the different paint projects available from the tools option in Purple Mash. Demonstrate picking one of the many options to create a design. Explain that students will be picking their own paint project, and when they are ready, they can print their work.

Activity
Students create one or more of their own paint projects. Once students finish, they can print their work.

Plenary
Ask students to come to the front to share their (printed) work with the rest of the class.

Lesson 2 & 3
Use a pen tablet to create digital art

Introduction
Introduce students to the Wacom pen tablet, explaining that this is a tool we can use to create artwork on the computer. Point out that it is easier to use a pen tablet to create art on the computer than using a mouse because the pen tablet imitates the experience that we have when we are holding a real pen.

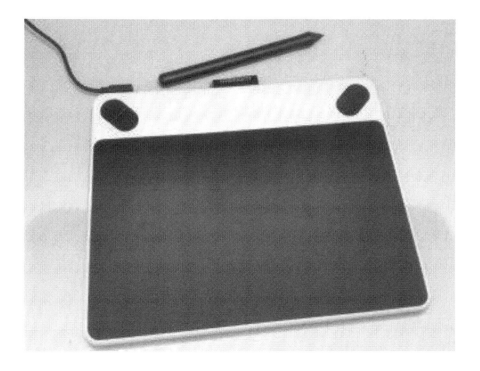

Then show students this video about how to create a seascape (https://www.youtube.com/watch?v=vOzQGCBuqec) using the Wacom tablet and ArtRage Lite software.

Activity
Students should use the ArtRage Lite software to spend these two lessons first creating a seascape and then creating their own, unique piece of digital artwork. Students may print their work when they have finished.

Plenary
Invite students to share their artwork with the rest of the class. Were there any techniques or tools from ArtRage Lite that worked particularly well? Discuss these with the students.

Lesson 4
Explore an online encyclopaedia

Introduction
Ask: what is an encyclopaedia? Elicit that an encyclopaedia is a book that contains lots of information about many different topics. The most popular encyclopaedia on the web is Wikipedia. Today we will be using the Online Infant Encyclopaedia. Explore this software with the students, and write up on the board the web address for students to type into their browsers: www.parkfieldict.co.uk/infant

Activity
Ask students to explore a particular topic using the encyclopaedia, e.g. the oceans. Students should read the information and complete the activities available.

Plenary
Put up one of the activities from the topic that students have been researching. Invite volunteers to come up to the front to answer the questions.

Lesson 5
Research Brazilian artists

Introduction
Explain that students will use this lesson to find out about famous Brazilian artists. They will decide on a style and artist that they like and attempt to emulate one of their paintings using the Wacom pen tablets for the following lesson.

They will search for one or more of the artists below from "Google Images" to see paintings by the different artists. Display this list for everyone to see, and demonstrate how to use Google Image search to look for paintings by these artists.

- Romero Britto
- Cândido Portinari
- Anita Malfatti
- Beatriz Milhazes
- Hélio Oiticica
- Lygia Clark
- Otavio and Gustavo Pandolfo
- Ferreira Louis Marius
- Aldemir Martins
- Constancia Nery
- Vik Muniz
- Tarsila do Amaral

Students should save their favourite image into their folders (Right click – Save image as).

Activity
The children should investigate one or more of the artists from the list above with the aim of choosing at least one favourite image by the end of the lesson. Once students have found a favourite image they should save it into their Pupil workspace folder. Remind students that they will be reproducing the picture they choose.

Plenary

Share the paintings that students have chosen by opening each student's folder on the interactive whiteboard. This will help to identify any student who did not manage to choose/save.

Lesson 6
Recreate chosen artwork using the Wacom pen

Introduction
Following the previous lesson, explain that students will be attempting to recreate their favourite artwork using the Wacom pen tablet.

Activity
Students should open up the artwork that they saved in their folders from the Google Image search they ran last lesson. They should then open up the ArtRage Lite software to start recreating the image. (If there are not enough Wacom pens to go around, students should try using the mouse and Microsoft Paint).

Plenary
Save and print finished work. To save their work from ArtRage Lite, students should click File > Export Image file. Invite volunteers to share their painting and recap on relevant vocabulary: fill, paint, straight line, undo, save.

Year 4 - E-Safety

Assessment focus area: Digital Literacy

Beginning (**Must**)	Developing (**Should**)	Mastering (**Could**)
Recall SMART rules for using the Internet.	Create a poster using Google Slides. Demonstrate an understanding about how to keep personal information private. Contribute to discussion about safer Internet use.	Articulate the purpose of using avatars online.

Lesson 1: Be careful when opening emails from strangers
Lesson 2: Recognise what is meant by personal information
Lesson 3: Create an online avatar
Lesson 4: Identify cyberbullying

Lesson 1
Be careful when opening emails from strangers

Introduction
In today's lesson, we will focus on what can happen if you open up emails from people you don't know. Then show children this video of What Should You Accept?
http://www.childnet.com/resources/the-adventures-of-kara-winston-and-the-smart-crew

Activity
Using this poster (http://www.kidsmart.org.uk/downloads/create-a-poster.pdf) as an example, ask children to design a better-looking poster using Google Slides.

Plenary
Check that children can explain the poster they have created.

Lesson 2
Recognise what is meant by personal information

Introduction
Ask: what is meant by personal information? Elicit that personal information is the details about you that only people you know or trust should know. Explain that we need to be particularly careful online about giving out personal information.

Show children this video http://www.childnet.com/resources/the-adventures-of-kara-winston-and-the-smart-crew/chapter3.

Activity
Ask children to explore the Cyber Cafe. As an extension, children can use a program like Inspiration to create a mind map of facts they learn about keeping personal information private online.
(https://www.thinkuknow.co.uk/8_10/cybercafe/Cyber-Cafe-Base/)

Plenary
Review what children have learnt about personal information and keeping it private on the Internet.

Lesson 3
Create an online avatar

Introduction
Ask the children if they know what an avatar is. Explain that online avatars are graphical representations of ourselves, which we use in order to protect our personal identity. We may not want other people to have our photograph, so it is safer for children to use avatars.

Activity
Children use the buildyourwildself (http://www.buildyourwildself.com/) website in order to create their own avatar.

As an extension, children should copy and paste the image into Word. Underneath the image they should write, using their own words, why we use avatars online.

Plenary

Make sure everyone understands the purpose of using an avatar - to protect their identity online. If there is time spare, show children these What Would You Do If (http://www.teachingideas.co.uk/sites/default/files/whatwouldyoudoif.pdf) questions. Discuss the different scenarios with the children.

Lesson 4
Identify cyberbullying

Introduction
Remind children about the e-safety assembly they saw the other day. Show them this cyberbullying video (https://www.youtube.com/watch?v=6FobM3ada90), discussing the different types of cyberbullying that took place. Then display the cyberbullying quiz, and complete it together as a class, asking them to raise their hands. (http://www.teach-ict.com/ks3/internet_safety/quizzes/internet_safety_quizzes.htm)

Activity
After children have completed the quiz, they should create a display with their top tips for staying safe online.

Plenary
Review what the children have learnt over this course of lessons about e-safety. Do children remember?

Year 4 - Co-authors

Assessment focus area: Digital Literacy

Beginning (**Must**)	Developing (**Should**)	Mastering (**Could**)
Join Google Classroom.	Access and submit work via Google Classroom. Embed their work onto the class Google Site.	Present their work to the rest of the class.

Lesson 1: Introduction to Google Classroom
Lesson 2: Create a Google Drawing
Lesson 3: Contribute a page to the class website
Lesson 4 & 5: Create a Google Slideshow about an explorer or adventurer
Lesson 6: Make a treasure island map using spreadsheets

Lesson 1
Introduction to Google Classroom

Introduction
(Make sure that you have created a Google Classroom beforehand). Introduce the children to Google Classroom, modelling how to access it. Explain that Google Classroom is a platform to distribute and collect in work. Show the students how to join the Google Classroom using the join code, which you will need to display on the interactive whiteboard.

Create a new assignment on Google Classroom by writing up these three tasks below on Google Slides - make sure that each student has a copy.

Task 1 - Complete the missing words and use arrows to label the different parts of the computer.

m.....................

p....................

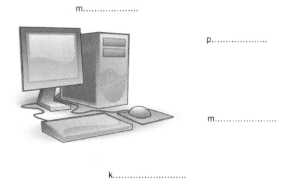

m.....................

k.........................

Task 2 - Complete the sentences.

The screen that displays pictures is called the

The computer's memory and machinery is in the

We control the computer by using the mouse and the

Task 3 - Design your own computer using the different shapes.

Activity
Once they join, children should access the assignment that you have added to the Google Classroom.

Plenary
Make sure that everybody knows how to submit their assignment. You can have a look at this video (https://www.youtube.com/watch?v=m6wtRI8gw_o) if they are unsure.

Lesson 2
Create a Google Drawing

Introduction

Show the children how to access the Google Drive and create a new Google Drawing. (*Click New > More > Google Drawing*). Explain to students that they will need to create a drawing of what they think of when they think "explorer". Here is an example.

Model how to send shapes to the back, e.g. when creating a background. When they have finished their drawing, explain to students that they will need to make sure that it is shared so that anyone in the British school can see their picture - show the children how to share their work.

Activity
Students should go ahead and create a Google Drawing. More able learners can create a background and label their drawing using arrows and text function.

Plenary
Explain to students that they do not need to save their work when using Google Apps, as their work is automatically saved. Review some examples of students' pictures.

Lesson 3
Contribute a page to the class website

Introduction
Ask: what is a website? Elicit that a website is a set of web pages joined together, which people can use in order to find information online. Discuss with the children different websites that they view regularly. Explain that in today's lesson we'll be working together to create a class website using Google Sites.

Demonstrate creating a Google Site. Create a page within the website called Adventurers & Explorers. Then model how to create another page with the Adventurers & Explorers section using the name of an example student. In this example student's page, model how to embed a Google drawing of an explorer from last lesson's activity.

Activity
Children create a page on the class Google Site. They should then embed their drawing from last lesson into this page. Underneath their drawing, children should write a few sentences about their imaginary explorer. As an extension, children can make more drawings to embed into the Class Google Site. (Make sure that you remind children to click Share > Get shareable link - this will ensure that their drawing is viewable by others on the class Google Site).

Plenary
Check that everyone was able to make a page on the class Google Site. Ask: can anyone in the world view our website? Explain that the sharing permissions on our school network prevent anyone from outside the school community being able to view this website. Ask why this might be important, linking to e-safety.

Lesson 4 & 5
Create a Google Slideshow about an explorer or adventurer

Introduction
Show children how to access Google Slides from their Google Drive. Explain that they will be making a short slideshow to embed into the class website. Using an example, demonstrate how to add and format text into Google Slides. Email students the URL, http://www.ducksters.com/biography/explorers/. Here they will find information about different explorers. *Assign the template for the Google Slide using Google Classroom.*

Activity
Students must create a presentation in Google Slides, which provides a mini-biography of one explorer. The presentation should include a title with the name of the explorer and it should answer the following questions:

- Where was the explorer from and when was he/she born?
- What did the explorer love to do?
- An interesting fact about the explorer
- Some information about the explorer's family
- Problems that the explorer overcame
- What did the explorer achieve?

Plenary
Ask children to share some interesting facts they have discovered about the explorer/adventurer they are investigating.

Lesson 6
Make a treasure island map using spreadsheets

Introduction

Explain that explorers and adventurers generally use maps to find where they want to go. Maps come in all shapes and sizes, but usually have something called grid references to pinpoint a location on the map. Show children an example of an imaginary treasure island map on Google Sheets:

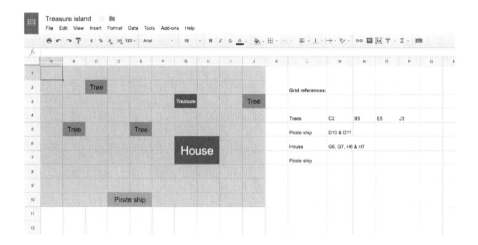

Ask children to identify different grid references for various artefacts on the map, e.g. Tree, treasure, boat, etc. *Assign the template for the Google Sheet using Google Classroom.*

Activity

From Google Drive, children create their own imaginary treasure island map using Google Sheets - the map should be 10 x 10. They should include cell references on the spreadsheet for the location of the different artefacts. (Make sure that you remind children to click Share > Get shareable link - this will ensure that their drawing is viewable by others on the class Google Site.)

Once finished, children should submit their work via Google Classroom and embed their map into the class Google Site on their page, as shown in this example. Make sure that students share this by clicking Get shareable link.

Plenary
Review children's work. Was everyone able to embed their maps into the class Google Site? Did all children write down the grid references of the different artefacts they placed on the map?

Year 4 - Develop a Simple Game (Bright Sparks)

Assessment focus areas: Computer Science

Beginning (**Must**)	Developing (**Should**)	Mastering (**Could**)
Design an interactive game. Create sprites using the Paint tool in Scratch. Put Scratch blocks in the right order.	Use the if/then/else block correctly. Be able to connect the Makey Makey to the computer. Debug (correct mistakes) in the game. Predict what will happen in a game by looking at the code.	Create a game controller using the Makey Makey. Include sound in the game. Use variables to work out a score. Use a countdown timer. Explain how the algorithm of the game works.

Lesson 1: Introduce the Makey Makey
Lesson 2: Use playdoh to create game controllers
Lesson 3: Identify an algorithm as a set of instructions
Lesson 4: Use algorithms to create a basic program in Scratch
Lesson 5: Create the graphics for a program in Scratch
Lesson 6: Programming Sprites
Lesson 7 (Extension): Add some interesting effects to the Scratch game

Lesson 1
Introduce the Makey Makey

Introduction

Explain that a Makey Makey is a circuit board, which we will use to learn more about electricity. Ask: does anyone know what a circuit board is? Elicit that a circuit board is an object that carries electricity from one point to another. Because many things like computers and toy cars need power to work, they have circuit boards inside to make sure that the electricity gets to the places where it needs to go.

The Makey Makey is a special type of circuit board because we can easily use it to connect the computer to other objects that conduct electricity. By using the Makey Makey, we will learn about the different parts of a circuit (the power source, wires, input and output) and how the circuit interacts with the computer.

Show students this video (https://www.youtube.com/watch?v=rfQqh7iCcOU) of the Makey Makey in action. Then demonstrate how to connect the Makey Makey to the computer in the following steps:

Step 1: Plug in USB
Small side of USB cable plugs into Makey Makey, big side plugs into computer.

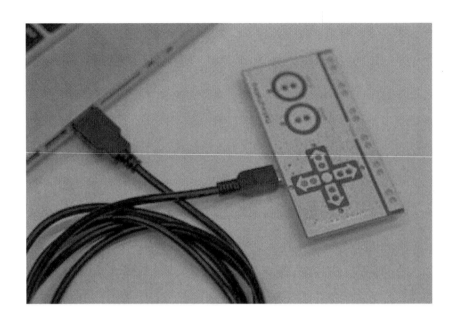

Step 2: Connect to Earth
Connect one end of an alligator clip to "Earth" on the bottom of the front side of Makey Makey.

Step 3: Connect to Yourself
Hold the metal part of the other end of the alligator clip between your fingers. You are now "grounded."

Step 4: Play some Makey Makey drums!
While you're still grounded, have open the drums website (http://makeymakey.com/bongos), and demonstrate playing the drums using the Makey Makeys. Invite a volunteer to be part of your circuit and demonstrate how, by touching the volunteer's nose, you can still play the drums.

Activity
(Children should connect the Makey Makeys themselves in this lesson). Using Google Classroom, share with students the following online activities for them to use in order to explore how the Makey Makeys work:
Bongos (http://makeymakey.com/bongos)
Piano (http://makeymakey.com/piano)
MK-1 (https://ericrosenbaum.github.io/MK-1/)
Canabalt (http://www.adamatomic.com/canabalt/)

Scratch Piano (https://scratch.mit.edu/projects/2543877/)
Tetris (https://scratch.mit.edu/projects/2543877/)
Sound Effects (http://ronwinter.tv/drums.html)
Flash Flash Revolution
(http://www.flashflashrevolution.com/FFR_the_Game.php)
Chamber Music Piano
(http://www.flashflashrevolution.com/FFR_the_Game.php)

Plenary
Invite students to come up to the front to demonstrate what they have learnt. In preparation for next lesson, ask students to bring in a few fruits or vegetables. We will be exploring how different foods can be used as controllers.

Lesson 2
Use playdoh to create game controllers

Introduction
Explain that many different materials can conduct electricity, including playdoh! In this lesson, we will be using the playdoh to make game controllers.

Activity
Following the steps taught in the previous lesson, children should set up their Makey Makeys and connect them to the playdoh. (This activity can be adapted to use fruits and vegetables instead). Once connected, students can experiment again with the different Makey Makey game sites available.

They may like to test out their game controller with this game: https://scratch.mit.edu/projects/31583772/

Plenary
Discuss children's experiences with the Makey Makeys. Are there other materials we could use to make game controllers?

Lesson 3
Identify an algorithm as a set of instructions

Introduction
Start the lesson by playing a quick game (5-minutes) of Simon Says. (For example, Simon says "Stand up", Simon says "stand on one leg", Simon says "freeze", etc.)

Stop the game and ask children what Simon is doing - he is giving instructions. Does anybody know what we call the instructions that we give to a computer? When we talk about computers, we call instructions "algorithms". Algorithms are really important because they are needed to make programs. Ask the children to provide some examples of different computer programs that they use (e.g. computer games, email and websites) - make sure everyone understands that all of these programs are built using algorithms.

Individual Activity
Introduce children to Frozen game (let them watch the 3-minute video first) (https://studio.code.org/s/frozen/stage/1/puzzle/1).

Make sure that children understand that they will be using algorithms to play this game, which are sequences of instructions to make Elsa move.

Plenary
Bring up the BBC website (http://www.bbc.co.uk/guides/zqrq7ty) for children to see. Referring to examples from the web page, discuss key examples of algorithms and show children video of Nate following an algorithm to make a fireball.

Lesson 4
Use algorithms to create a basic program in Scratch

Before children begin, they will need to sign up for a Scratch account with their school email.

Introduction

Introduce Scratch to pupils. Show pupils the cat who is our sprite in Scratch. Explain that we are going to create a program in Scratch to control the cat. From the 'motion' and 'looks' tab add a series of commands as can be seen in the screenshot below. Think aloud as you are choosing these by talking through the selection of instructions and what you want the character to do e.g. he will move forward then rotate then. Note – deliberately include repetition in these commands as shown below. Click on the commands to explore the outcome of the program with your pupils.

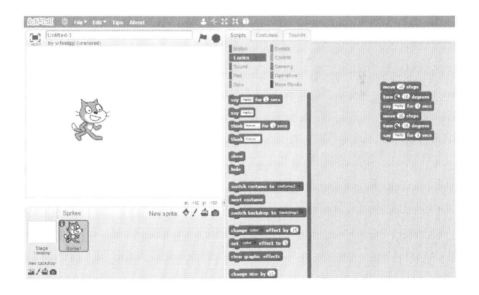

Activity

Ask pupils if they notice anything about the program you have written (prompt them to think back to first part of lesson). Establish that there is repetition in the program. Explain that we can shorten this code using a repetition/loop command. Can anyone see where this might be available with the control tab of Scratch? (Repeat command within 'Controls'). Demo using this to shorten the code i.e. place it around the repeated set of instructions and set the number of repeat times to 2. Note – to remove any unwanted commands simply click and hold them and move them outside the programming area. Run this program by clicking the play arrow and check the character does exactly the same as before.

Partner work: Pupils should now have time to experiment writing simple programs in Scratch. It is recommended they use the following quite simple commands but which have editable elements to them.

This session will ensure pupils become familiar with using the Scratch programming environment before the start to write more complex programs over the following weeks.

Extension: children use the Makey Makeys to control their sprites.

Plenary

Display a selection of the programs which pupils have produced. For each example of work shown, ask pupils to consider what the outcome will be before pressing play. This will help to develop pupils' ability to 'read code'.

Lesson 5
Create the graphics for a program in Scratch

Introduction/Activity

Begin by playing The Electrician Game (https://scratch.mit.edu/projects/70808416/#player) with the children. Explain that this is a simple Scratch game in which the electrician has to collect tools from around the city. Then show children "inside" to see the code, which runs this game - they will be using today's lesson to begin making something similar. (It does not need to be an electrician game - this is just one possible idea!)

Remind children about the Scratch interface from last lesson, going over the main features:

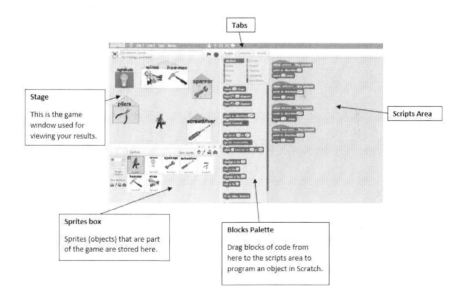

In today's lesson children will be making the background and sprites using the paint tool within Scratch.

Creating a sprite or background takes you to a Paint window, (see below) where you draw your object. The paint tools are similar to MS Paint and should be fairly intuitive.

You also have the opportunity to load a sprite by clicking the button next to the new sprite button, or alternatively you can import a picture by using the "Import" button from within the paint window. A background is simply the background to your game. A sprite is an object that moves within the game. It is important to ensure that pupils are familiar with all of this before they start.

For this game, the following sprites (objects) have been created:

Children may choose to create more or less sprites than shown here - it is entirely up to them. Pupils can design their own or import them from the Internet.

They will need to design a Sprite 1, which collects all the other sprites. In the case of this game, Sprite 1 is an electrician.

Plenary
Review how children got on. Who imported their sprites? Who designed their own sprites and background? Which was easier and why? The can then have a look at other "electricity" themed projects on the Scratch website, for example this model of an electrical circuit (https://scratch.mit.edu/projects/11486153/). Encourage the children to always look at the code that makes these programs.

Lesson 6
Programming Sprites

Introduction/Activity

Once you have all the graphics completed, we can program the Sprite 1 to move. Select the Sprite 1 in the sprite window and create the following scripts:

These 4 scripts are for the movement of the player. When an arrow is pressed the character will point in a direction and move 10 steps. You can click the flag to test it works.

On each of the objects to collect, create this script:

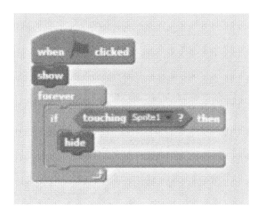

It is important to add the "Show" command to the start of this script as this will make the object reappear once the game has been restarted. This is called a "Condition" and these will be used throughout all the games. This script makes use of a "conditional if". This makes the game continuously check whether a condition has been met. In this case, has the collect object touched Sprite 1? If it has, everything below the 'if' will be executed in order.

Extension: children use the Makey Makeys to control their sprites.

Plenary
Check that everyone has created a main sprite, which is able to move around the board collecting all the objects. Ask if anyone has "bugs" (things that don't work properly) in their program. Were there any common bugs that children encountered when writing their code?

Lesson 7 (Extension)
Add some interesting effects to the Scratch game

Introduction
In this lesson children will begin to make their code more complex by adding some special effects. Open up the game (https://scratch.mit.edu/projects/70808416/#editor) and demonstrate how to change the code to add sound effects and speech bubbles.

Begin by showing how to add a sound effect by dragging the "play drum" code from the sound blocks into the code for one of the sprites:

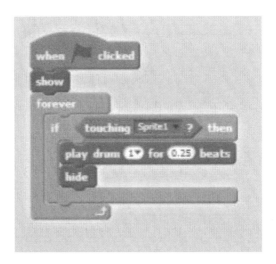

Ask the children if anyone can you show you how to make the main sprite say "Yippee!" when he collects one of the objects. The code should then be changed again to look like below:

Activity

Children should improve their code by adding similar visual effects to those demonstrated in class. For those who still haven't finished their game from last lesson, they should work on finishing this.

After 15 minutes stop the children and get them to swap seats with the child next to them. They should change one or two things in their partner's code. After they swap back again, it is up to the creator of the game to isolate the problem and fix it. This can then be used as a way of assessing pupils' ability to problem solve and debug code.

Extension: children use the Makey Makeys to control their sprites.

Plenary

Discuss the importance about what the children have been doing. Why do you think learning to code might be so important? Show children the video (https://www.youtube.com/watch?v=nKlu9yen5nc).

Year 4 - Survey Design

Assessment focus areas: Digital Literacy & Information Technology

Beginning (**Must**)	Developing (**Should**)	Mastering (**Could**)
Create a list of survey questions. Use Google Forms to create a survey.	Recognise what makes a good survey question and what makes a bad survey question. Create a presentation based on the survey results.	Understand some ethical and legal implications in survey design. Present survey results to the rest of the class.

Lesson 1: Complete an online survey & brainstorm your own survey questions
Lesson 2: Develop survey questions
Lesson 3: Create an online survey and send
Lesson 4: Copy & paste result charts onto Google Slides
Lesson 5 & 6: Complete Google Slide Presentation

Lesson 1
Complete an online survey & brainstorm your own survey questions

Introduction

Ask: what is a survey? Explain that a survey is tool we use to collect information from people. It contains a series of questions, which people answer. ICT can provide us with a powerful means to send surveys out to many people at the same time. Children will be creating their own survey to find out about a particular topic - but first, they are going to complete a survey that you send them using Google Forms.

Demonstrate creating and sending a Google form to the students - from the Google Apps in Gmail, simply click on Forms:

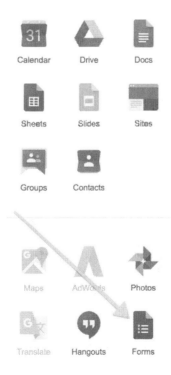

Once the form is complete, click on Edit this form on the top right-hand side, and then click on the blue button, **Send form**. Make sure that you type in your class email, and send this survey to your class.

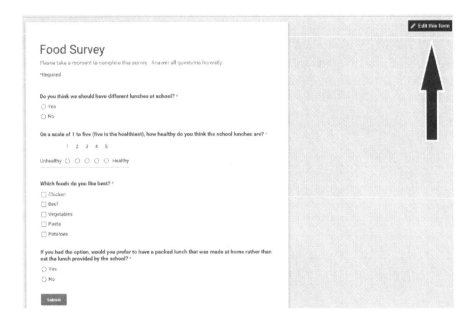

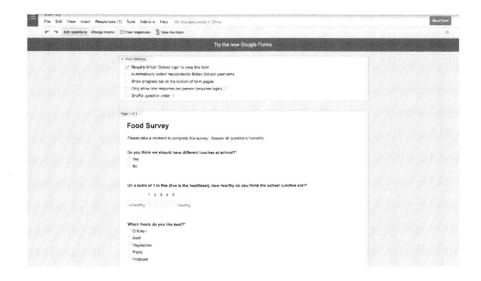

Activity

Students return to their computers and log into their Gmail where they will have received a link from you to complete the Google Form survey. Once students complete this survey, they can begin brainstorming and writing their own survey questions using Google Docs. These questions can be related to the IPC unit or to do with an area that interests the student.

Plenary

Review the results of the survey with children. (Click on Responses > Summary of Responses.) Go through each survey question, looking at any charts. Discuss what we have found out from using this survey. What could be improved about the survey?

Lesson 2
Develop survey questions

Introduction
Discuss with the children that survey questions need to be thought through carefully. Show them these survey questions:

1. What is your full name and address?

2. What is your age? Tick the correct answer:
   0 to 10
   11 to 20
   21 to 30
   31 to 40
   40 +

3. What is your favourite fruit?
   Kiwi
   Pineapple

4. Why don't you like homework?

5. What do you like most about school?

Go through each question with the children, asking them which ones they think are good survey questions and which ones are bad survey questions. Highlight poor survey questions and make sure children understand why (e.g. ambiguous questions, loaded questions, requests for identifying information, questions that do not make sense, results that will be hard to analyse, etc.)

Activity
Children should write up to 10 different survey questions in Google Docs. These questions can be related to the IPC unit or to do with an area that interests the student. As an extension, children can upload their questions to the Class Google Site.

Plenary
Ask for volunteers to share the survey questions that they have created. Discuss which questions are good questions and which ones might need to be changed.

Lesson 3
Create an online survey and send

Introduction
Now that children have written up their draft survey questions from last lesson, it's time to put these on a survey template. Using some of children's survey questions from last time, model creating a survey on Google Forms. Show the different questions that can be included, such as text, paragraphs, multiple choice, scales and grids. Show how to give the form a title and a description, discussing what would be appropriate for these fields. When writing questions, discuss the difference between the help text and the question text. Draw the children's attention to the *Make required question* box, and discuss the advantages and disadvantages of this.

Activity
Ask the children to login and create their survey questions using Google Forms. As an extension activity, ask the students to add images next to their survey questions. When children have finished writing up their survey, they can send it out to five other children (**refer to the groupings for the survey on the following page or choose your own groupings**). Within their groups, students can then complete the surveys of other students from their group.

Plenary
Discuss the results children got from their surveys. Ask children what the best survey questions were, and why?

Lesson 4
Copy & paste result charts onto Google Slides

Introduction
Show children again the survey that they filled out a few lessons ago. Model how to access and analyse the results of the survey, using Google Forms' built-in tools, under Summary of Responses. Point out that the charts provide us with a useful way of seeing visually everybody's responses.

Model how to copy and paste the charts from Google Forms into Google Slides and provide a short summary of what each result shows.

Activity
Children copy and paste the charts from Google Forms into Google Slides. They should write a short summary of what each chart shows.

Plenary
Discuss with children the importance of keeping the results of the surveys anonymous when publishing online. Explain that this is because of something called 'data protection', which means that we must respect other people's privacy and that the answers people give to our survey questions should remain anonymous.

Lesson 5 & 6
Complete Google Slide Presentation

Introduction
Explain that the results presented should look professional. It is therefore important that children put the finishing touches to their presentations, including a title page, subtitles, and so on.

Activity
Children should finish their presentation, making sure that it looks professional. Encourage them to insert pictures to accompany the questions, use WordArt for titles and ensure they have a description for each survey question.

Plenary
Once children have finished their presentations, give them the opportunity to share these with the rest of the class.

Year 4 - Toy Design

Assessment focus area: Digital Literacy & Information Technology

Beginning (**Must**)	Developing (**Should**)	Mastering (**Could**)
Identify the difference between inputs and outputs.	Create a text-based algorithm that sets out simple instructions.	Create an algorithm for each one of the different inputs on the picoboard.
Use Google Drawings to design a toy.	Write a script in Scratch to control their simulation.	

Lesson 1: Find out about input devices and output devices
Lesson 2: Design a toy
Lesson 3: Design the toy in Scratch
Lesson 4 & 5: Program the toy simulation
Lesson 6: Use the Picoboard

Lesson 1
Find out about input devices and output devices

Introduction
Explain to the students that they are going to become toy designers. They will be designing their own interactive toys and then using Scratch to make an on-screen simulation of their toy.

Begin by asking the students to name as many different computers, or devices containing computers, as they can. Encourage them to think broadly (ideas might include washing machines, microwaves, digital alarm clocks and mobile phones.) As you elicit these ideas from the students, note them down on the whiteboard.

Then show the students this video https://www.youtube.com/watch?v=WhISokrfeDA, which explains the difference between input and output devices.

Activity
Using Google Slides, students will produce a display, one column to illustrate input devices and another column to illustrate output devices. You can show students this example below. Make sure that students print their work for display.

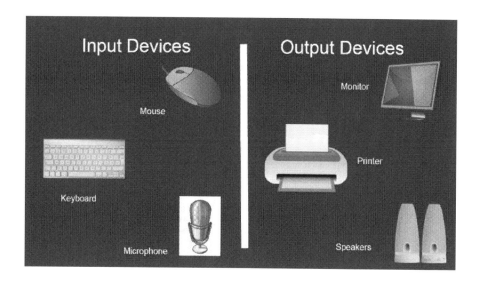

Plenary

Review students' understanding of inputs and outputs. Using NetSupport, display a student's work on the whiteboard. Ask: are there any other input or output devices that we could add?

Lesson 2
Design a toy

Introduction

Explain that in this lesson, students will begin to put together a design for their toy using Google Drawings. Show them this example of one made earlier:

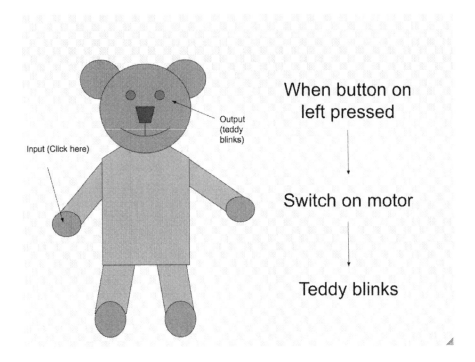

As shown in the example, encourage the students to think of their toy in terms of a computer system, which accepts an input (such as a button being pressed), runs a stored program (set of instructions), and produces an output (such as a sound, lights or a motor to produce some kind of movement.)

Activity

Using the example as a guide, students open up Google Drawings to create their own version of a toy design. Remind them that it is better to start off with a simple idea and then build on it, rather than do something too complex initially. On one side of their page, the students should create a design for their toy, and on the other side, an algorithm (set of instructions) should be written that shows how the toy responds to an input.

Plenary

Using NetSupport, review some examples of students' work. Discuss how effective the various ideas might be, and if any of the designs need tweaking.

Lesson 3
Design the toy in Scratch

Introduction
Explain to the students that they now need to think about how they translate their ideas for the inputs, outputs and computer program from their toy design into a virtual simulation created in Scratch.

Show students the example again from last lesson of a toy design, and then show them how this could look in Scratch here:
https://scratch.mit.edu/projects/15364900/#player.

Point out that each one of the system components of the toy (each part that the computer controls) is drawn as a separate sprite.

Activity
Students go ahead to design their toy in Scratch. If the students have planned any inputs or outputs that cannot be simulated in Scratch, give them time to change or simplify their designs.

Plenary
Discuss the designs the students have created in Scratch. Review the text-based algorithms that students came up with the last lesson. Have children remembered to keep their designs and algorithms simple like the example?

Lesson 4 & 5
Program the toy simulation

Introduction
In this lesson, students will begin to program their design in Scratch, using blocks of code that stimulate their toy's inputs and outputs. The input could be a mouse click for example (to stimulate pressing a button). Outputs, such as movement (which would normally be caused by a motor), could be stimulated using movement commands for individual components or by costumes showing different poses.

Your teacher demonstration can include the following steps:

Step 1: Increase size of sprite so everyone can see the toy clearly.

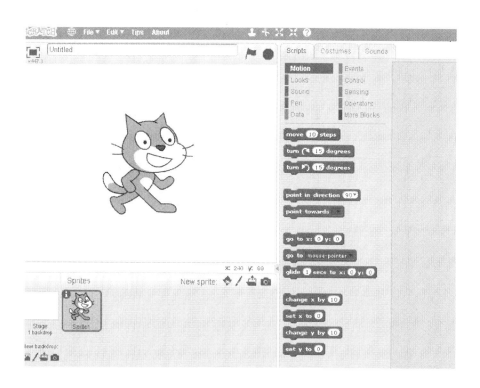

Step 2: Create a new sprite, which should be a button. (This new sprite will be your input device.)

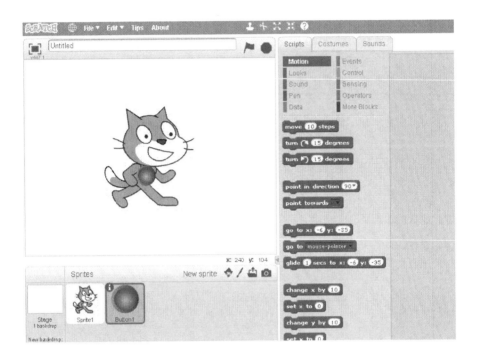

Step 3: Click on Events under the Scripts tab, drag across 'when this sprite clicked' block and 'broadcast message1' block.

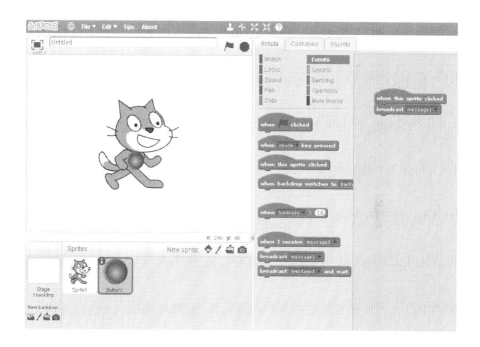

Step 4: Click on the original sprite. Select the blocks below to demonstrate an output for when the button is clicked.

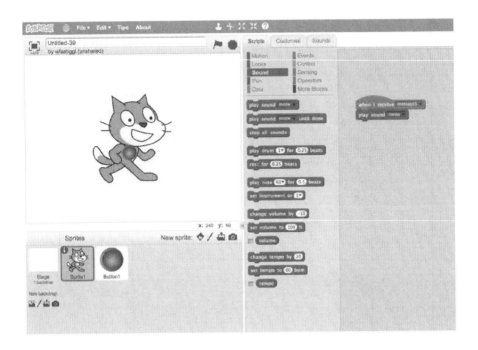

Step 5: Demonstrate other examples of possible inputs and outputs, e.g. broadcasting another input message 'when this sprite clicked' that causes the toy to change colour.

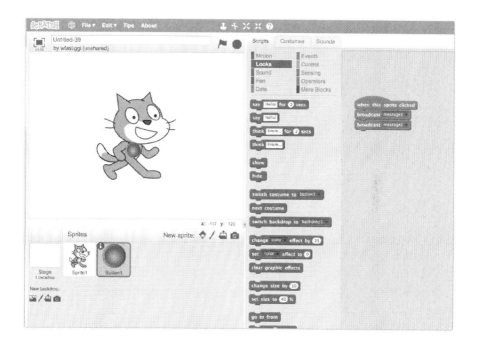

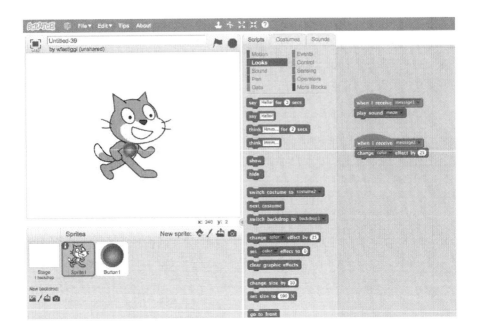

Ask students: what is the input for the toy? What is the output? Elicit that pressing the button is the input and the output (in this example) is the toy making a sound and changing colour.

Activity

Students should write scripts in Scratch to control their sprites. The script should contain an input (broadcast message for one sprite), e.g. a button and an output for the other sprite.

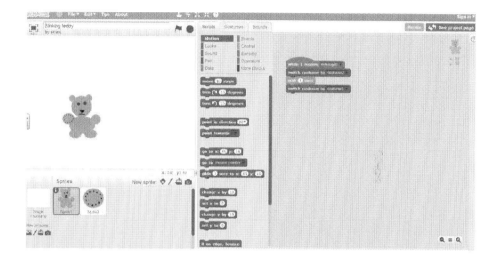

Plenary

Check that everyone has been able to create a simulation for a toy with an input and output. Using NetSupport, display some examples on the whiteboard.

Lesson 6
Use the Picoboard

Introduction
Note - for this lesson, students will be using the offline version of Scratch (Scratch 1.4 installed on the computers, which is compatible with the Picoboard). Explain that the Picoboard is a sensor board, which enables Scratch to respond to events happening outside of the computer. Connect the Picoboard to the computer via the orange USB cable.

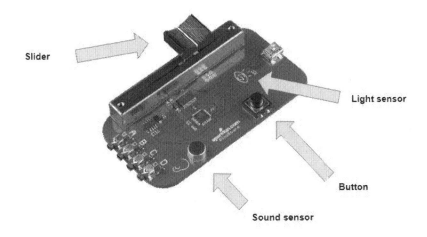

Slider

Light sensor

Button

Sound sensor

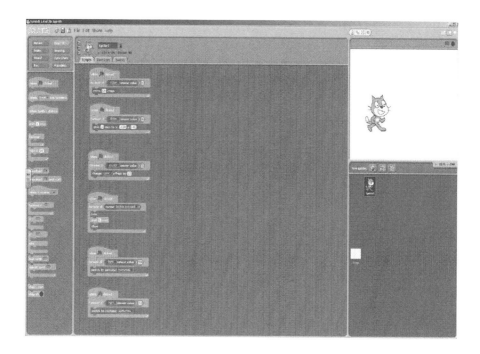

Point out the different sensors on the Picoboard as shown on the image. Once connected, demonstrate how to create a simple event in Scratch using the Picoboard. From the Sensing palette, begin by dragging over the block, '*slider sensor value*'. Explain that when the slider is moved on the Picoboard, we want the sprite on the screen to move as well. To do this, we need to put the '*slider* sensor value' block inside a greater than (>) block.

The final block of code should look like this:

```
when 🏳 clicked
forever if < slider ▾ sensor value > 1 >
    move 10 steps
```

Then demonstrate how, when the slider is moved, the sprite moves across the screen. Ask: how can we make sure that the sprite returns to its original place? Elicit that we need to create a new block of code that says, 'forever if *slider* sensor value' = 0 go to these specific coordinates. The block of code should look something like this:

```
when 🏳 clicked
forever if < slider ▾ sensor value = 0 >
    glide 1 secs to x: -128 y: -43
```

Continue to go through several different examples that use different inputs from the Picoboard (sound, button pressed, light):

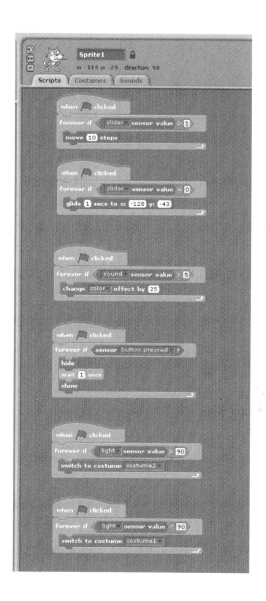

Ask in each case: what is my input? Elicit from the students that the button, slider, light sensor and sound sensor are all examples of inputs; the output is what happens to the sprite as a result of the input.

If time, invite volunteers to come up to the front to create their own examples using different sprites, and for each sprite, making use of a different sensor:

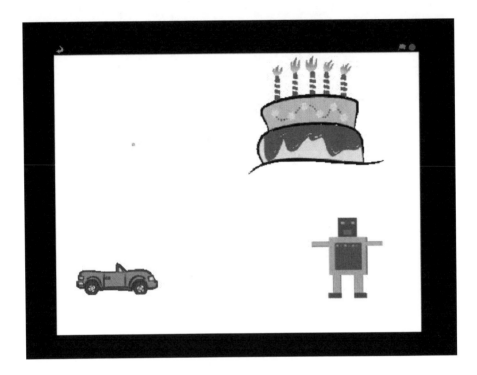

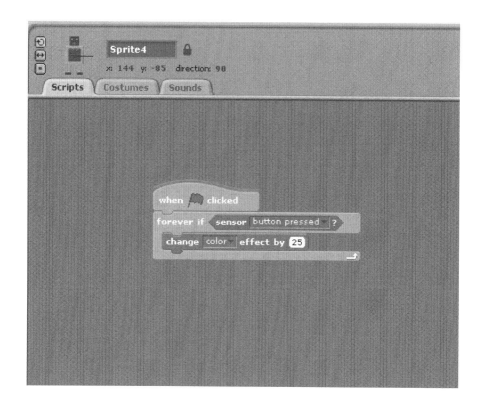

Activity

Students should create a new Scratch program (using Scratch 1.4), which responds to four of the Picoboard's inputs: light, sound, the button and the slider.

Plenary

Open NetSupport, and ask for volunteers to showcase their work. Check students' understanding of inputs and outputs as they relate to the Picoboard and sprite.

Year 4 - Animation

Assessment focus area: Digital Literacy & Information Technology

Beginning (**Must**)	Developing (**Should**)	Mastering (**Could**)
Use ABCYa to create a simple animation. Animate one or more characters using the Puppet Pals app on the iPads. Create a 10-second stop motion animation.	Define what a stop motion animation is. Download ABCYa animation as a GIF file and save in student folder. Download Puppet Pals animation to iPad's camera roll and upload to the Google Drive. Create a 30-second stop motion animation and upload to the Google Drive.	Have a clear storyline for the stop motion animation. Add appropriate sound effects and/or voiceover to the stop motion animation.

Lesson 1: Create a simple animation
Lesson 2 & 3: Create an animation using Puppet Pals
Lesson 4: Complete a storyboard
Lesson 5 & 6: Create a stop motion animation

Lesson 1
Create a simple animation

Introduction
Explain to the students that in this unit they will be creating a series of animations. Show them this animation as an example:
https://www.youtube.com/watch?v=HUngLgGRJpo

Discuss with the students what they liked and disliked about the animation. What do they think works well for holding the viewer's attention? In this lesson, students will create their own simple animation using the ABCYa website
http://www.abcya.com/animate.htm.

Demonstrate using ABCYa to create a short animation. Click Go > Model how to add a background, insert characters and duplicate slides.

Activity
Students should go ahead and create their animation using ABCYa. For the second part of the lesson, demonstrate how to export the animation by clicking on Export as GIF:

Once the animation has finished exporting, click on Save. Then show the students how to upload this animation to their Google Drive and share with you.

Plenary
Using NetSupport, showcase a student's work on the display.

Lesson 2 & 3
Create an animation using Puppet Pals

Introduction

Model for the students how to use Puppet Pals. Demonstrate selecting a backdrop, character(s) and selecting music. When everything is in place, record the voiceover whilst moving the characters on the screen. Explain to the students that their animation should have a beginning, middle and end, and it should not go on for any longer than five minutes.

Activity

Students create their animation using Puppet Pals. For added creativity, encourage students to insert their own headshot images into the animations. When students have completed their final animation, help them to save the animation to the iPad's camera roll. From there it can be uploaded to the student's Google Drive.

Plenary

Invite students to play back their animation for the rest of the class to watch. Discuss what works well and what could be improved.

Lesson 4
Complete a storyboard

Introduction
Ask: what is a stop motion animation? How is this different from other animations that we've seen? Elicit from the students that stop motion is a technique, which requires physically moving an object in small increments and each time taking a snapshot. By doing so, the object appears to move on its own.

Then show students this Wallace & Gromit animation, explaining that we call this type of animation "stop motion": https://www.youtube.com/watch?v=2igRcGxlshA&feature=youtu.be

After watching the video, discuss what makes a good stop frame animation, for example, using figures, including a set, good lighting and including dialogue and music.

Look at two more examples with the students for inspiration:
https://www.youtube.com/watch?v=RGeanX-xBYo
https://www.youtube.com/watch?v=_wT5TKvmLTM

Activity
Share with students the Stop Motion Storyboard Template via Google Classroom. Organise the students into pairs, explaining that one person from each pair is responsible for sharing the Stop Motion Storyboard Template with their partner. Once all pairs have shared access to their storyboard template, they should work together to plan their stop motion animation. (**Note: You may need to demonstrate how to insert drawings and add rows to the table.**)

Plenary
Invite some volunteers to share their storyboards with the rest of the class.

Lesson 5 & 6
Create a stop motion animation

Introduction
Explain that we will be using the iPad app, iStopMotion to create a short stop motion animation. Students will begin by creating a set (out of Lego, card and/or plasticine) and use basic objects from around the classroom (Lego, plasticine or playdoh is ideal) to make their stop motion animation. Ideally, a good animation should last at least 30 seconds. Using AirPlay, demonstrate how to use the iStopMotion app on the iPad, reminding students that the most realistic movements occur when there is only a little movement between each frame.

Activity
Students should work in pairs to use iStopMotion to create their stop motion animation. (**iPads should be labelled with students' names, so they can quickly find their project for next lesson.**) Allow 2 to 3 lessons in order to complete this activity. When students have completed their stop motion animation they should save it to the iPad's camera roll and upload it to their Google Drive.

Plenary
Invite students to present their stop motion animations to the rest of the class, and encourage students to give sensible peer feedback.

Year 4 - Digital Imagery

Assessment focus area: Digital Literacy & Information Technology

Beginning (**Must**)	Developing (**Should**)	Mastering (**Could**)
Open up photos saved in a shared folder. Create a Google Slide and share with the teacher.	Demonstrate the ability to make several different edits to photos, including cropping, the PhotoFix feature and Filter Effects feature.	Show evidence of using more advanced features of PhotoPlus, including use of the Magic Wand Tool and Cloning Tool.

Lesson 1 - Crop a digital photo
Lesson 2 - Use the PhotoFix feature
Lesson 3 - Use Filter Effects feature
Lesson 4 - Edit groups of pixels
Lesson 5 - Use the Clone Tool

Lesson 1
Crop a digital photo

Introduction

In this lesson, students will learn about cropping. Find out if any students know what the term "crop" means when we're talking about editing digital photos. Explain that cropping is a technique used to remove unwanted parts of photos. The user highlights the part of the photo they want to keep and the rest of the photo is deleted. If used well, cropping can often improve photos.

Discuss these three examples of how cropping can be used:

1. Cropping can be used to focus on the subject of the photo and correct any framing mistakes. Click on the Crop Tools icon and use the mouse to drag a rectangle over the desired area of the photo for cropping:

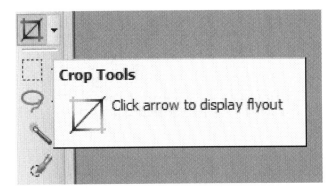

When this is done, double click on the desired area to crop the photo.

Using the rule of thirds, we can imagine that our photo is split into thirds. When you crop the photo, place the focal point (in this case, the boy at the front) where the grid lines cross.

2. The QuickShape Selection Tool allows you to select a range of different shapes in which to crop photos.

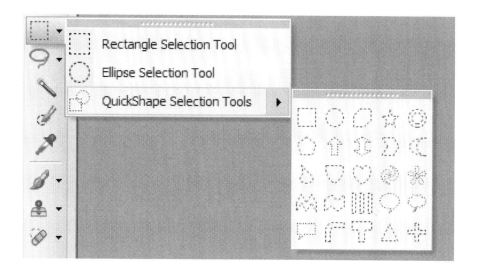

When this method is chosen and the area is selected, you need to double click on the area, then right click and select 'Crop to selection'.

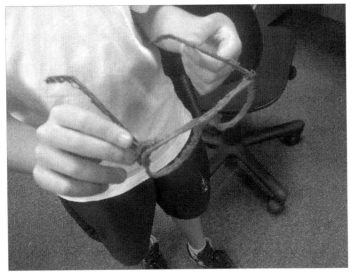

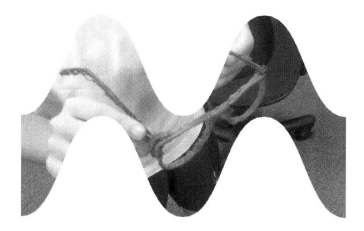

After showing students these three examples, introduce them to the pixabay website (https://pixabay.com/). Explain that all the images on here do not have a copyright licence and are therefore free to use or share.

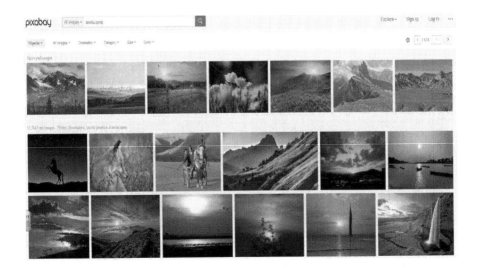

When the chosen image is found, right click on the image and click 'Copy image'.

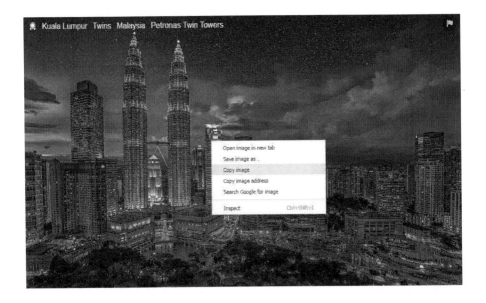

Then from PhotoPlus, click Edit > Paste > As New Image.

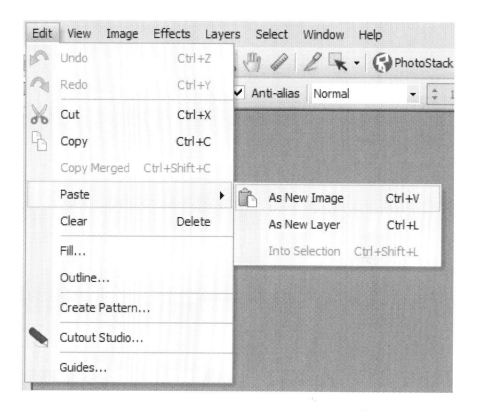

Activity
Students should create a new Google Slide to place their images. (**Students will be using this same Google Slide for all the lessons in this unit**). Using the Pixabay website, students should choose three landscape images to copy and paste into PhotoPlus, cropping each image one at a time. At least one of the images should be cropped using the standard crop tool and one using the quickshape selection tool. After an image is cropped, students should copy the image from PhotoPlus and paste it onto their Google Slide.

Plenary
Students should share their work with the teacher. Invite volunteers to present their work to the rest of the class.

Lesson 2
Use the PhotoFix feature

Introduction
Explain that another of PhotoPlus' built in features is
PhotoFix. This feature allows users to create different versions
of their photographs.

Show students these examples of the PhotoFix feature:

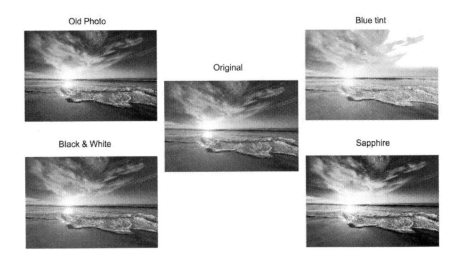

In this lesson, explain to students that they will first use
Google Advanced Image Search in order to find an image of a
landscape that has a minimum size of 800 x 600 and is free to
use and share. Remind students of why it is important to only
search for images that are free to use and share. Demonstrate
the steps to do this:

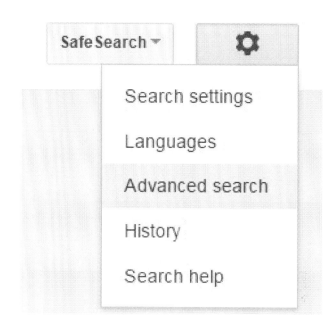

(Alternatively, you can just get the students to use the Pixabay website again.)

Activity
Students should follow these steps to search for a landscape of their choice and then copy it. Once they have done this, students should open up PhotoPlus > select Paste > As New Image.

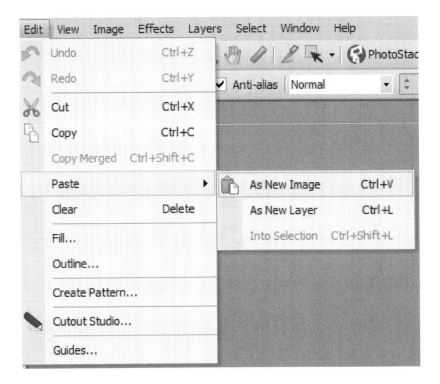

Once students have the image of their choice in PhotoPlus, they should experiment using the PhotoFix on their photo. As students create different versions of their photo using the PhotoFix feature, they should copy and paste these into a Google Slide and share with the teacher.

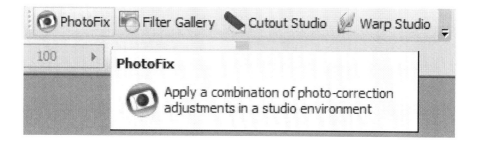

Plenary

Open up students' Google Slides that have been shared with you. Showcase the different effects students have created using the PhotoFix feature.

Lesson 3
Use Filter Effects Feature

Introduction
Begin this lesson by reminding students how to perform a Google Advanced Image search (or the Pixabay website). Invite a volunteer to demonstrate how to search for an image of a landscape that has a minimum size of 800 x 600 and is free to use or share. Then check that everybody remembers how to copy this image and open it up in PhotoPlus.

Explain that in this lesson we will use filters to completely change a photo's appearance. Demonstrate how to apply a filter to a photograph (1. click Filter Gallery > 2. select the desired filter).

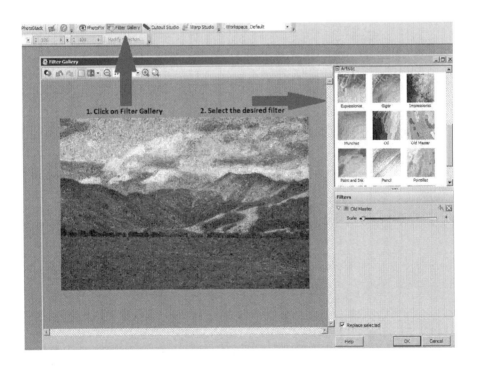

Activity
Students should perform a Google Advanced Image Search to find an image of a landscape that has a minimum size of 800 x 600 and is free to use or share. Once students have decided on an image, they should create three different versions using the Filter Gallery and present these images on their Google Slide.

Plenary
Share a few of the students' work with the rest of the class. Which filters do students think are most effective and why?

Lesson 4
Edit groups of pixels

Introduction

Explain that images are made up of thousands of pixels. A pixel is the smallest element of an image that we can edit. If we select groups of pixels therefore, we can edit smaller parts of a photo separately.

By using the Magic Wand Tool and clicking on a picture, we can select whole areas of a photo. In this lesson, students will practise using the Magic Wand Tool on a beach scene image. Begin by showing students a beach scene image similar to the one below.

Then demonstrate the following: removing the sky, colouring the sky and colouring the sea. (These instructions can be shared via Google Classroom).

1. Removing the sky:
   - First, convert the background to a layer. Right click on the Background in the Layers tab, select Promote to Layer and click OK.
   - Next, click on the wand tool and set the tools options as shown:

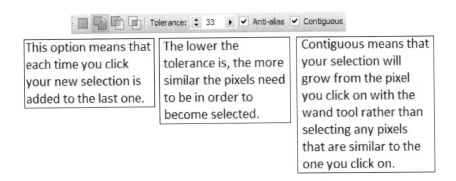

This option means that each time you click your new selection is added to the last one.	The lower the tolerance is, the more similar the pixels need to be in order to become selected.	Contiguous means that your selection will grow from the pixel you click on with the wand tool rather than selecting any pixels that are similar to the one you click on.

- Then, click on the bottom of the sky. Keep clicking on deselected areas until the whole sky is selected.
- Finally, select Edit and then Cut.

2. Colouring the sky:

- Once the sky is deleted, right click on the selection and click Deselect.

- Click on the Flood Fill Tool , select the desired colour and click in the area where the sky should be.

3. Colouring the sea:
- Follow the previous steps for removing the sky and colouring the sky in order to be able to colour the sea.

Activity
Students should open up the beach scene from the Media Centre and experiment with using the Magic Wand Tool to create different versions of the image. These images can be copied and pasted onto their Google Slide.

Plenary
Invite students to show their work to the rest of the class.

Lesson 5
Use the Clone Tool

Introduction

Ask: what does the word clone mean? Elicit that in digital photo editing, cloning means copying pixels.

Explain to the students that the clone brush  allows you to select part of a photo and then use this as a paint brush on another area. If carefully done this tool allows you to improve the quality of your photo by removing imperfections.

Show students this a spot the difference example in which the Clone Tool has been used.

Demonstrate how to do this activity:

Step 1 - Click on the Clone Tool  and make the following changes to the menu options below:

Opacity: ↕ 67 ▶ % Brush: ● Size: ↕ 35 ▶ | Flow: ↕ 62 ▶ % ✔ Airbrush ☐ Aligned

Step 2 - Move the cursor over the area that you want to copy and press down the Alt key. Use short drags and mouse clicks over the area you are changing until the colours have been blended in.

Activity
Using a pre-selected image, students should experiment with using the Clone Tool to create their own Spot the difference puzzle on a new Google Slide. As an extension, students can search for new images to add to their Google Slide.

Plenary

Look over examples of students' work. Invite volunteers to identify the difference between the before and after photos.

Year 5 - E-Safety

Assessment focus area: Digital Literacy & Information Technology

Beginning (**Must**)	Developing (**Should**)	Mastering (**Could**)
Articulate rules to follow in order to stay safe online.	Identify and define spam, cyberbullying and viruses. Explain what netiquette means and how we can demonstrate good netiquette online.	Use WordArt to enhance Safer Internet displays.

Lesson 1: Identify the risks associated with using digital communication
Lesson 2: Recognise key hazards of using the Internet, including spam, cyber-bullying and viruses
Lesson 3: Recall strategies on how to stay safe online
Lesson 4: Demonstrate good netiquette

Lesson 1
Identify the risks associated with using digital communication

Introduction
Brainstorm with the children some of the risks associated with using the Internet, and show them this Jigsaw video: https://www.youtube.com/watch?v=_o8auwnJtqE Discuss the mistakes that the girl (Becky) made in it that helped the stranger find and follow her. Elicit from the children that if we put personal information online, a stranger can piece together lots of small facts about us (like a jigsaw puzzle).

Activity
Using Google Classroom, provide each child with a blank Google Slide template. On the Google Slide, children should do the following:

- Record what digital communication technologies they use themselves.
- Write us some rules that Becky should follow to help her stay safe online in the future.

Plenary
Review what the children have learnt in this lesson. What are the risks associated with digital communication tools? How can we minimise these risks?

Lesson 2
Recognise key hazards of using the Internet, including spam, cyber-bullying and viruses

Introduction
Ask children for their help to match the terms for spam, cyber-bullying and virus to their definitions.

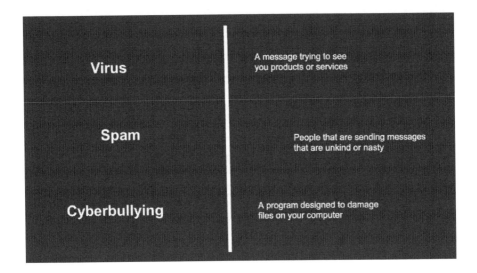

Activity
Write down the following scenario questions on the board:
1. A friend sends you an email attachment you're not sure of. What should you do?
2. You get an email from a stranger telling you that you've won a prize and they want to phone you to tell you what it is. What should you do?
3. Someone you've only met online asks to come and visit you. What should you do?
4. Someone on a social networking site says something unpleasant to you. What should you do?

Ask children to complete their answers on four separate slides independently, including relevant images.

As an extension, children can refer to the Sorted website and create a poster about Internet Security (http://www.childnet.com/sorted/index.aspx).

Plenary
Check children have included a range of strategies in their responses like:

- **the importance of checking email attachments are safe to open** (e.g. by confirming with the sender or using an anti-virus program like the free *Microsoft Security Essentials*);
- **the need to just delete any spam messages** as they are likely going to be unwanted adverts or messages asking you for personal information to claim a prize you've apparently won (which likely won't exist and your details will be used for fraudulent reasons/to send more spam instead);
- **to never agree to meet up with strangers you've only met online** in case they aren't who they say they are and you are put in a vulnerable position;
- **to always report incidents of cyberbullying immediately to a trusted adult**, keeping the received messages as proof/evidence and not responding to the bully with a nasty comment back (which makes you as bad as them).

Lesson 3
Recall strategies on how to stay safe online

Introduction
Ask children if they can remember some of the potential problems we can face when using the Internet. Write these down on the board.

Activity
In today's lesson, children can explore the Cyber Café website (https://www.thinkuknow.co.uk/8_10/cybercafe/Cyber-Cafe-Base/). Explain to the children that they will need to complete the activities on this website in order to reinforce all the things that we have been learning in a more interactive way.

Plenary
Finish with a short discussion on **the reasons why you should only communicate and join age-appropriate websites**, highlighting points such as: you won't be breaking the rules of the site by lying (stress the word 'lying') about your age, there will be more safety controls in place to make it less likely that you become the victim of cyberbullying and the material on them is going to be more appropriate for your age (e.g. not contain images which could offend/upset you).

Lesson 4
Demonstrate good netiquette

Introduction
Ask the children if anyone knows what etiquette means? Explain that it just means we are polite with other people, showing them respect. Ask: what do you think netiquette means then? Elicit from the children that netiquette refers to how we behave online.

Show children this video (https://www.youtube.com/watch?v=NYJydonwb3A about netiquette. Brainstorm with the children some ideas for good netiquette, e.g. don't write all in capitals, re-read what you write before you send it, ask permission before posting things about friends, etc.

Activity
Ask children to produce a display using Google Docs, outlining a set of rules for following good netiquette. Once finished and checked by the teacher, these displays can be printed.

Plenary
Review the rules everyone has written for their display. Are there any other rules that we can add? Why is it important that we follow these rules?

Year 5 - Digital Portfolios

Assessment focus area: Digital Literacy & Information Technology

Beginning (**Must**)	Developing (**Should**)	Mastering (**Could**)
Set up a digital portfolio using Google Sites.	Upload images and ICT work onto digital portfolio. Use WordArt to enhance Google Slide.	Demonstrate understanding of copyright. Search for and use royalty free images.

Lesson 1 & 2 - Make a digital portfolio using Google Sites
Lesson 3 & 4 - Create a Google Slide related to IPC unit
Lesson 5 & 6 - Explore Google Earth & take screenshots to upload to digital portfolio

Lesson 1 & 2
Make a digital portfolio using Google Sites

Introduction
Explain to children that in this lesson they will be making a digital portfolio where they will be storing all of their work. Show the students this video (https://www.youtube.com/watch?v=GAiFH0rxMPY) on how to set up a digital portfolio using Google Sites. (It would be helpful if you create your own Google Site to show students).

Activity
Students now create a Google Site following the instructions from the video - this will be their digital portfolio.

Your digital portfolio should include:

- Your first name and last name
- A homepage with a brief introduction, for example 'Welcome to my digital portfolio. This is a space where I showcase my learning in Computing & ICT'
- Three sections (Computer Science, Digital Literacy and Information Technology)
- A logo (see one of the website links below to build a logo - just use free version of software)
        http://cooltext.com/
        http://www.flamingtext.co.uk/

As an extension, students can start adding work they have produced from the previous unit, E-Safety, to their digital portfolio.

To insert images (logos) or documents, follow these steps:

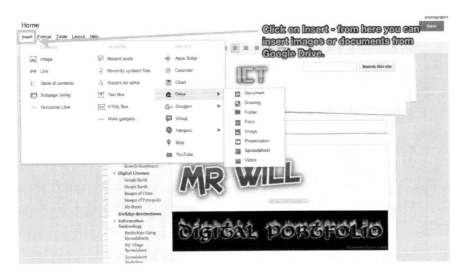

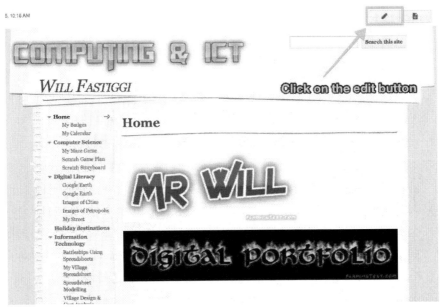

Plenary

Review some of the children's digital portfolios. Have they all managed to embed logos into their portfolios? Have they started to upload work to their portfolios?

Lesson 3 & 4
Create a Google Slide related to IPC unit

Introduction
Explain to the students that they will create a short presentation related to the IPC unit. When finished, they will have to embed this presentation into their digital portfolio.

Model how to create a Google Slide (From Google Drive, click *New > Google Slide*).

Then demonstrate how to insert WordArt onto the front page (*Insert > WordArt*).

Explain to students that when searching for images, they need to make sure that these are free to use or share.

You can show this video (https://www.youtube.com/watch?v=APuwNPI4-EE) on how to perform an Advanced Google Image Search in order to find free to use or share images.

Activity
Students begin creating their presentation using Google Slides. Using an Advanced Google Image Search, the students should search for only free to use or share images relevant to the IPC topic in order to add to their presentation.

Plenary
Using NetSupport, ask for volunteers to share their Google Slides. What works well? What could be improved?

Lesson 5 & 6
Explore Google Earth & take screenshots to upload to digital portfolio

Introduction
Use the interactive whiteboard to show the children how to access Google Earth (*Start > Google Earth*). Explain that children will need to find their street using Google Earth. They should then take three screenshots of their home location using different views. Model how to take a screenshot (*Cntrl + Prnt Srn*), then past this screenshot (*Cntrl + v*) into Microsoft Paint. Demonstrated how to then save the pasted screenshot and upload this to the digital portfolio.

Activity
Children explore Google Earth, taking three screenshots of their home to upload to their digital portfolio.

If children finish this, demonstrate how to switch to flight mode – select "Enter Flight Simulator" from the Tools menu and then select your aircraft of choice and a starting location. The SR22 is a slower plane and easier for beginners. Access the flight simulator's help screen by pressing Ctrl-H. They can also explore Mars and the moon in flight simulator mode.

Plenary
Check all children have been able to take screenshots and upload these screenshots of where they live onto their digital portfolios.

Year 5 - Researching

Assessment focus area: Digital Literacy & Information Technology

Beginning (**Must**)	Developing (**Should**)	Mastering (**Could**)
Search and gather information from online sources.	Create a news report template in Microsoft Publisher (or a similar program). Use WordArt to create a news headline. Add a border and image.	Demonstrate understanding of copyright when searching for images. Identify examples of a good news report (e.g. Catchy headline, use captions, answering key 'w' questions: what, when, where, why, etc.)

Lesson 1, 2 & 3 - Research information online and create a news report

Lesson 1, 2 & 3
Research information online and create a news report

Introduction

Explain to students that they will be writing news report related to one of their subjects of study. Model how to open Microsoft Publisher (or a similar program), insert a text box, add a headline, insert a picture and add a border. This introduction can be spread over two lessons. By the final lesson, students should gather enough information in order to compose their news report.

Activity
Students go ahead and create the template for their news report. They should use appropriate search engines online (e.g. Kiddle.co, KidRex.org) and write the report using their own words.

Plenary
Review students' work. Invite volunteers to present what they have written to the rest of the class. Which graphic features are most effective at drawing attention to the reports?

Year 5 - Spreadsheets

Assessment focus areas: Digital Literacy & Information Technology

Beginning - **Must**	Developing - **Should**	Mastering - **Could**
Search for free to use or share images. Embed some examples of work into the digital portfolio.	Make relevant comments on digital portfolios. Collect a range of free to use or share images and display these on the portfolio. Make a design using Google Sheets.	All work completed needs to be showcased on the digital portfolio by use of screenshots and include some written reflection. Calculate costs of materials for several buildings using spreadsheets. Design a village (two or more buildings) using Sketchup.

Lesson 1 - Collect a portfolio of free to use or share images of different holiday destinations
Lesson 2 - Introduction to spreadsheets
Lesson 3 - Design a holiday resort using Google Sheets
Lesson 4 - Calculate costs of building a holiday resort
Lesson 5 - Enter simple formulae into a spreadsheet
Lesson 6 - To use =SUM to add up numbers in a spreadsheet

Lesson 1
Collect a portfolio of free to use or share images of different holiday destinations

Introduction
Explain to the children that in this session they will create a display on their digital portfolio of five holiday destinations around the world. Ask: can we take any image from the Internet to use on our digital portfolio? Praise any student who says no, we can't use any image we want because lots of images that we come across online are protected by copyright.

Then show children the following tutorial video about the Copyright of images:
https://www.youtube.com/watch?v=APuwNPI4-EE
Ask for a volunteer to model searching for a free to use or share images of a village. When this image is found, demonstrate how to copy and paste the image onto a Google Doc. When this is done, explain that it is good practice, where possible, to credit the image to its creator. Remind the students to then embed this Google doc into their digital portfolios.

Activity
Using a Google Advanced Image Search, the students should search for free to use or share images of villages. They should copy and paste these images onto a Google Doc, which they can call 'Holiday Destinations'. Remind children to reference the images. Once they have embedded their Google Doc, 'Holiday Destinations' into their digital portfolio, underneath they should write a few sentences about the different holiday destinations they have selected.

Plenary
Review children's work. Has everyone found images of different holiday destinations, which are free to use and share?

Lesson 2
Introduction to spreadsheets

Introduction
Explain to the children that they will be learning to use spreadsheets. Ask: does anyone know what spreadsheets are? A spreadsheet is a document that is divided into rows and columns, which is used to solve problems involving lots of numbers. Today we will be learning about spreadsheets by playing the game, battleships.

Show the children this video (https://www.youtube.com/watch?v=ToZ6vhCiF_s) to give them an idea of how the game works.

Activity
Student should create their own battleships template and position their ships on the template, using this sheet as an example:

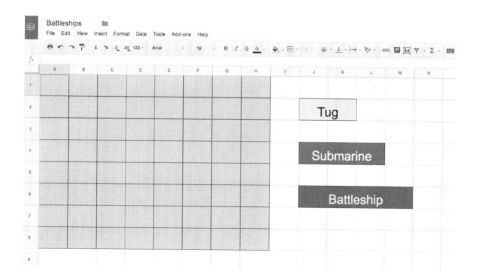

Once everyone has finished, you will be ready to play battleships! Call out cell references - if a student has one of his or her ships in one of the cell references that you call, then the student should change the colour of the vessel to black and the vessel is sunk.

Plenary
When you have finished the game, make sure that all students embed their battleships template into their digital portfolio.

Lesson 3
Design a holiday resort using Google Sheets

Introduction
After they have played a session of battleships, demonstrate how to design a holiday resort using Google Sheets. You can show them this example:

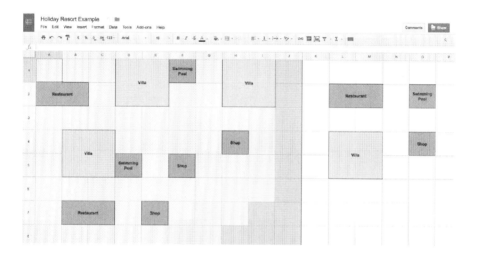

They can include the following items: villas, shops, restaurants, swimming pools, beach, sea.

Activity
Students should design a plan for their holiday resort (10 x 10 cells) using Google Sheets. (Make sure that you provide each student with a template using Google Classroom). Encourage children to think about roads and access points. They should label all the buildings, use colour and embed their sheet into their digital portfolio. Explain to students that next lesson they will be calculating the costs to build their holiday resort.

Plenary
Referring to examples of the children's work, discuss what makes particularly good designs for a holiday resort, e.g. roads, restaurants near villas, plenty of shops to generate income for the local economy, etc.

Lesson 4
Calculate costs of building a holiday resort

Introduction

Explain to the children that before a holiday resort or even a single building can be built, the total costs need to be calculated. In this lesson, we will be using spreadsheets to calculate the costs of all the materials that you will need for your village based on designs from the previous lesson.

Note for teacher: Create a 'Building Materials Cost Analysis' template as illustrated in this example below. The layout and numbers can be adapted as you see fit. The important thing is to demonstrate using formulae to calculate all the costs for building a restaurant.

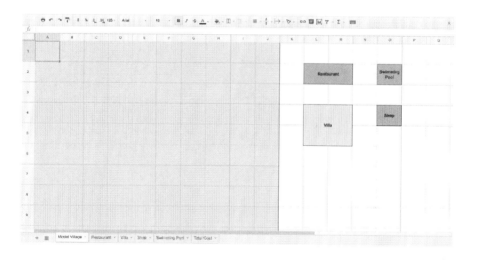

fx | Building Materials Cost Analysis

	A	B	C	D	E
1	**Building Materials Cost Analysis**				
2					
3					
4					
5	Material	Price (per unit)	Number of units needed	Cost	
6	Concrete	4	6		
7	Electrics	6	5		
8	Glass	7	6		
9	Metal	8	8		
10	Wood	5	5		
11	Plaster	4	4		
12	Plumbing	7	3		
13	**Subtotal**				
14					
15				Total Cost	
16	Number of restaurants to be built:				
17					
18					
19					
20					
21					
22					
23					
24					
25					
26					

+ ≡ Model Village ▾ | Restaurant ▾ | Villa ▾ | Shop ▾ | Swimming Pool ▾ | Total Cost ▾

Activity

Based on the children's holiday resort designs from last week, they should begin by calculating the total cost of building them. To do this they will continue to use the template provided from the previous lesson. (The total cost will depend on how many buildings they have in their design).

When students have finished this spreadsheet and calculated the total cost, they should embed the spreadsheet into their digital portfolio.

Plenary

Review children's work. Who designed the most expensive holiday resort? Who designed the cheapest? What made the holiday resort more expensive and what buildings would be best for the local economy?

Lesson 5
Enter simple formulae into a spreadsheet

Introduction
Explain and demonstrate that students can enter formulae into cells to help workout the answers. Demonstrate how to create formulae involving the four main operators (+, -, *and /) which can all be easily accessed using the numeric keypad) and emphasise how the answers to formula calculations will always appear in the cell where the formula was entered into. Point out the formula bar at the top where the formula used can be seen and how all formulae must begin with an =(equals) sign because it means 'here comes a formula' – without this the computer will mistake what you are typing as just text.

Activity
Using Google Classroom, send the children each a copy of 'The Gold Mine' (from Simon Haughton's website: http://www.simonhaughton.co.uk/2010/04/introducing-spreadsheets-week-1.html). In this task, they will need work out the answers to various calculations and if they are right, the cells will automatically turn gold. The file is organised into three worksheets which can be accessed by clicking on the tabs at the bottom: level 1 only contains additions, level 2 contains subtractions as well and level 3 contains multiplications and divisions as well.

Plenary
Play Snakes & Ladders competition between the boys and the girls.
http://www.what2learn.com/spreadsheet-game-ks3/

Lesson 6
To use =SUM to add up numbers in a spreadsheet

Introduction
Can you remember what the different parts of a spreadsheet are called? How do you work out a cell reference? What do you start all formulae with? Why should you enter formulae for calculations and not just type the answer in? (So the answer can update automatically if changes are made to the source data).

How would you add up lots of numbers in a spreadsheet? Point out that whilst using=B10+B11+B12+B13+ would produce a total; it would require a lot of typing and thus would be hard to spot any mistakes with in it. Introduce the use of =SUM(B10:B15) as a shorter way of adding up a series of numbers in a column, stressing the importance of the syntax.

Activity
Ask the children to load up the 'Race Points' spreadsheet (from Simon Haughton's website: http://simonhaughton.typepad.com/ict/introducing-spreadsheets/), which they will access from Google Classroom. Discuss what formulae would need to be entered and where to help determine which child received the most points. Give the children some time to work in the spreadsheet to determine who got the most points.

As an extension, children can create an imaginary shopping list of 20 items in one column and the price of each item in another column. They will need to calculate the total cost of all of the items.

Plenary
Check that the children all know how they could do lots of additions in a spreadsheet more quickly in the future.

Year 5 - Kodu

Assessment focus areas: Computer Science & Information Technology

Beginning - **Must**	Developing – **Should**	Mastering - **Could**
Create a setting in Kodu.	Take screenshots in Kodu to upload onto digital portfolio. Program the controls of one Kodu character to move left, right, backwards and forwards. Insert a timer in Kodu and create an enemy character that reacts to the main character.	Change the settings of characters in Kodu - e.g. to alter the blip reload rate and show the health bar. Evaluate the strengths and weaknesses of the game created.

Lesson 1 - Create a setting in Kodu and take screenshots
Lesson 2 & 3 - Program Kodu to move and collect objects to score points
Lesson 4: Program enemies that can shoot
Lesson 5: Develop the Kodu game
Lesson 6: Complete Kodu Maze Tutorials

Lesson 1
Create a setting in Kodu and take screenshots

Introduction

Explain that Kodu is an application designed to teach students programming skills. We will be using this application over the next few lessons to learn how to create a computer game. In this lesson, students will begin by designing a virtual world where their game will take place.

Open up Kodu and select New World. Show the students how they can add more land using the Ground Brush tool and how the Up/Down tool can be used to create hills or valleys:

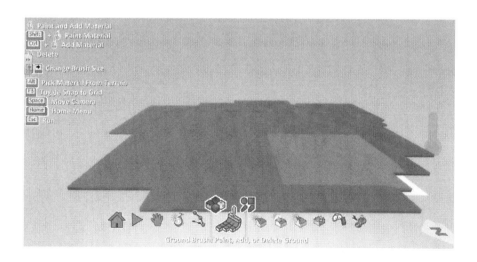

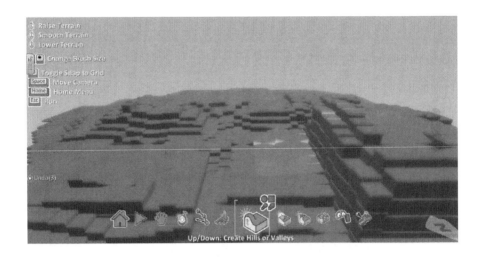

Finally, show the students how they can insert objects like trees into their world by clicking first on the Object tool, and then once an object is selected, right clicking on the place where they want the object to appear.

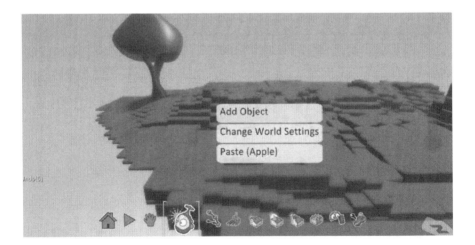

Activity
Students should go ahead to create the setting for their Kodu world. When they have finished, students should make sure

that they take screenshots of their world from different angles to upload onto their portfolios.

Plenary
Using NetSupport, display some of the students' worlds on the whiteboard. What types of world do students think would make a good gaming environment?

Lesson 2 & 3
Program Kodu to move and collect objects to score points

Introduction
In this lesson, we will insert an object to start programming. Explain that the game students create must involve one character collecting objects in order to earn points. Demonstrate inserting a Kodu character into the gaming environment and objects for the character to collect.

Model and try to elicit from the students how to carry out the following programming steps:
- Move the character using the arrow keys;
- Program the character to collect objects (e.g. an apple) and earn points each time an object is collected;
- When a certain number of points are earned, the game is won;
- Insert a timer, so that after a set time, the game ends.

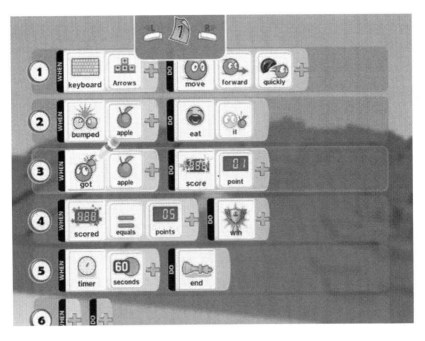

Activity
Students should work on programming a character for their game and inserting objects for the character to collect. They should make sure that once a certain number of the object if collected, the game is won. As an extension, students should insert a timer to make the game more challenging.

Plenary
Ask students to play each other's games so far. What worked well, and what could be improved?

Lesson 4
Program enemies that can shoot

Introduction

Ask the students for their ideas about what is needed in order to make their games more challenging. Elicit that they should insert an enemy character, which shoots at the main character the user controls. Model and elicit to the students the programming steps necessary to accomplish this:

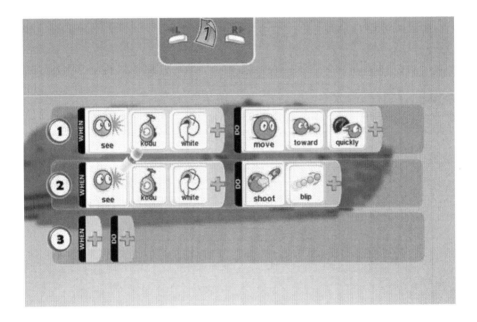

Ask for a volunteer to come forward to play the game so far. Students will notice that the game suddenly becomes very difficult because the enemy character (based on the programming above) shoots too fast. Demonstrate how to change the settings in order to alter the blip reload rate by right clicking on the Kodu character and clicking on Change Settings.

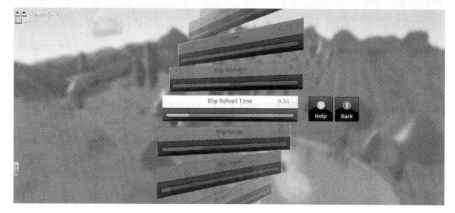

Activity

Students should insert and program an enemy to shoot at the main character. As an extension, ask students if they can work out how to display the main character's health and if they are able to display the countdown timer.

Plenary

Using NetSupport, display one of the game on the whiteboard. Ask for volunteers to play the game. What works well and what could be improved?

Lesson 5
Develop the Kodu game

Introduction
Based on feedback the students have received from their peers, explain that they should finish developing their game.

Activity
Once students have finished developing their game, they should take screenshot of each one of their kodu characters and the code they used, to upload to their digital portfolio.

Plenary
Discuss with the students what they learnt from developing a game in Kodu. If they could change their games, what would they do differently? What worked well, and what could be improved?

Lesson 6
Complete Kodu Maze Tutorials

Introduction
From the Kodu homepage, click on Load World, and explain that from here we can select challenges to complete. The students will be using the skills they have acquired over the last several lessons to test their programming skills in Kodu. Open Maze Tutorial 1, and ask for the students help to program Kodu to find Brodu.

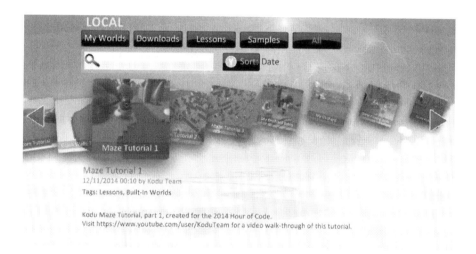

Activity
Students should complete Maze Tutorial 1, 2 and 3. As an extension, students can attempt other missions available of their choosing.

Plenary
Ask for a volunteer to demonstrate to the rest of the class how they completed Maze Tutorial 2. Make sure that the volunteer explains step by step the programming that is necessary.

Year 5 - 3D Modelling

Assessment focus areas: Digital Literacy & Information Technology

Beginning - **Must**	Developing - **Should**	Mastering - **Could**
Create a 3D model using Tinkercad. Show good digital etiquette when using Minecraft.	Build appropriate 3D structures in Minecraft. Embed some examples of work into the digital portfolio.	Create a design to be 3D printed.

Lesson 1 - Create a 3D version of your name in Tinkercad
Lesson 2 - Create a 3D design of an anchor
Lesson 3 - Design a model robot
Lesson 4, 5 & 6 - Use Minecraft to create a theme park made up of different 3D structures

Lesson 1
Create a 3D version of your name in Tinkercad

Introduction
Begin the unit by showing students this video about 3D printing:
https://www.youtube.com/watch?v=IS4Xw8f9LCc. Explain that 3D printing is becoming increasingly common, and it begins with creating a 3D design. Over the next few lessons we'll be learning how to use a program called Tinkercad. In today's lesson, students will use Tinkercad to create their name using 3D letters.

Show students how to create an account on Tinkercad: https://www.tinkercad.com/.

Then model for the students how to drag the 3D letters over to the workplane. Show students how to resize and reposition the letters.

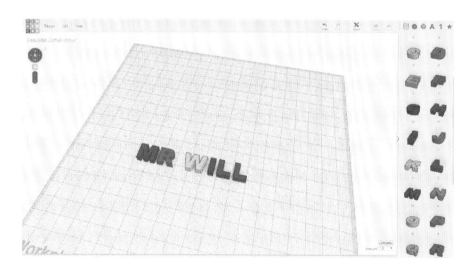

Activity
Students should go ahead and create a 3D design of their name. As an extension, they can explore and add additional 3D designs to the workplane. When finished, students should take a screenshot of their design in order to upload to their digital portfolio.

Plenary
Use NetSupport to review examples of students' work.

Lesson 2
Create a 3D design of a house

Introduction

Explain to the students that in order to develop some of the more advanced skills in 3D modelling, their task today will be to design a 3D house.

Begin by modelling for students the basics in how to drag appropriate shapes onto the workplane.

Part 1. Select and drag the red shape of "box" onto the workplane. The dimensions can be scaled as desired.

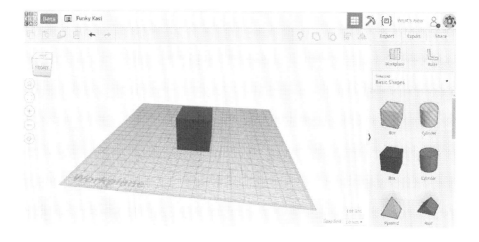

Part 2. Select and drag the shape of "Roof" onto the workplane. Demonstrate how to drag this shape over and above the cube by clicking and dragging the small cone that appears above the roof.

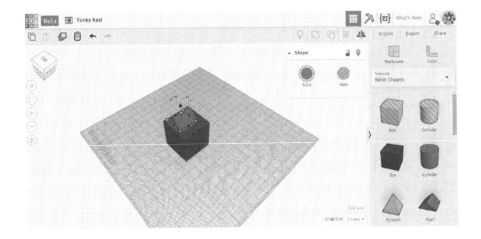

Part 3. Then reposition and resize the roof so that it covers the top of the cube.

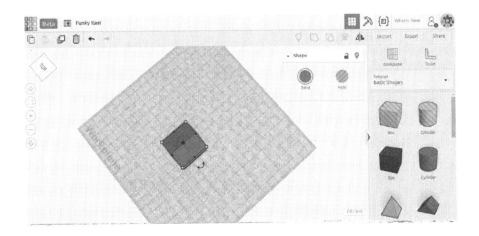

Part 4. Move around the two shapes by holding down on the right mouse button to see the shapes from the side.

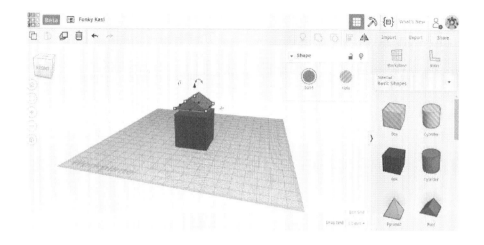

Part 5. Next, using the small cone icon that appears above the shape, drag the roof down so that it sits neatly on top of the cube.

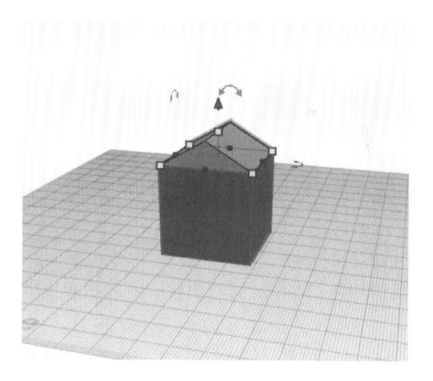

Part 6. Click on the 'box hole' shape from the tab section named 'holes'. Then, drag a new box hole onto the workplane.

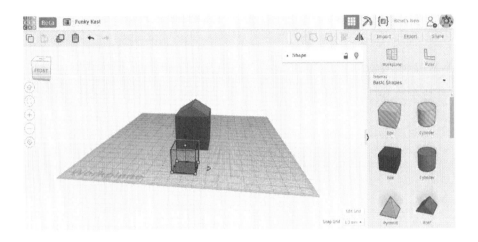

Part 7. Resize and reposition this shape as a small cuboid to move inside the cube – this will serve as the front door.

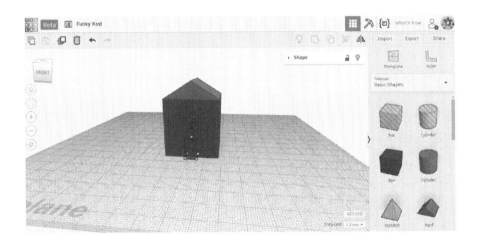

Part 8. Holding down the shift button, click on the three shapes to select them all. Then click on the "Group" button.

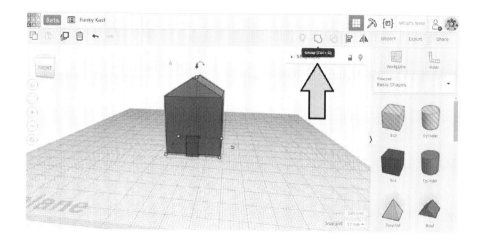

Part 9. This will group all the shapes together and will use the box hole shape to hollow out the doorway:

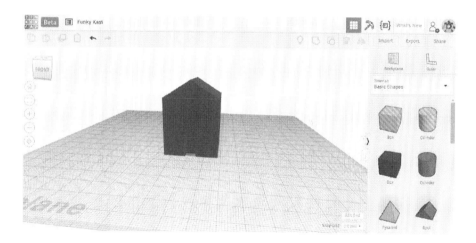

Part 10. Complete the same process to add windows to the house. Drag box hole shapes to be resized and repositioned as windows on the house. Once again, holding down the shift key, select all the shapes together and click "Group".

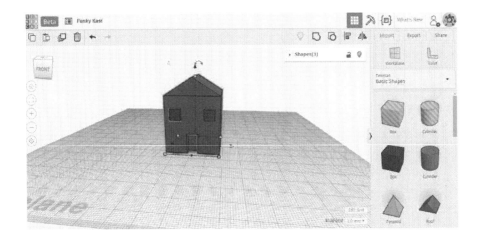

Part 11. Finally, you should end up with the shape of a generic house.

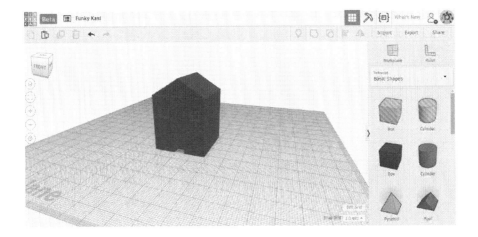

Activity
Students should create their own version of the generic house design. As an extension, challenge students to add additional features to their house design such as a chimney, balcony and garage.

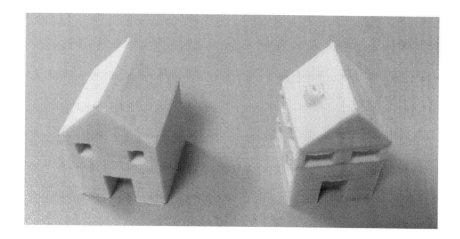

As pictured above, if your school has access to a 3D printer, you may like to turn this activity into a competition in which the best design gets 3D printed. Depending on the specifications of your 3D printer, make sure to give students the dimensions of how big they can make their design to ensure that it can be printed. Once a design has been picked, it simply needs to be downloaded from Tinkercad as an STL file and sent to the 3D printer.

Plenary
Review the designs that the students have produced. Invite volunteers up the front to demonstrate designing parts of their house again one step at a time.

Lesson 3
Design a model robot

Introduction
Now that students have obtained the necessary skills for using Tinkercad, set them a challenge! Students are to design a model for a robot. The robot should fit within the dimensions of 70 mm x 50 mm x 50 mm (length x width x height, respectively). Explain that the best design from each class will be 3D printed.

Look at some examples together with the students for images of robots:

Activity
Students design a model 3D robot and upload screenshots to their digital portfolio.

Plenary

Choose one of the students' models to 3D print.

Lesson 4, 5 & 6
Use Minecraft to create a theme park made up of different 3D structures

Introduction

Explain to the students that they will be working together to build a virtual theme park, using Minecraft. Note - some students will be very familiar with Minecraft, so it will be their job to help support students to help their classmates. This unit also builds on the learning of Minecraft that students should have covered during the 3D Modelling unit.

Teacher instructions for opening Minecraft:

<u>Step 1</u>
Open the Minecraft Server Tool on the teacher computer and select 'Start MinecraftEdu Server Launcher':

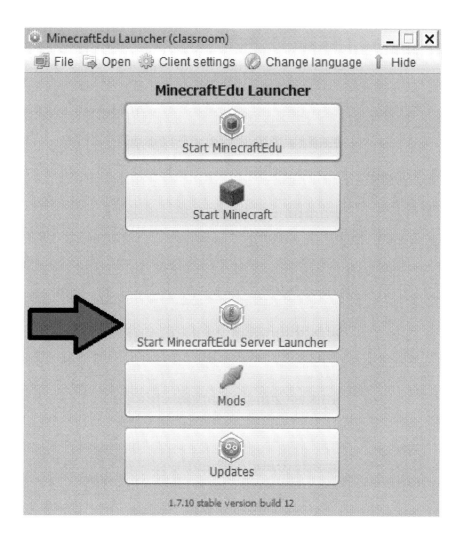

Step 2
Click 'Create New World'.

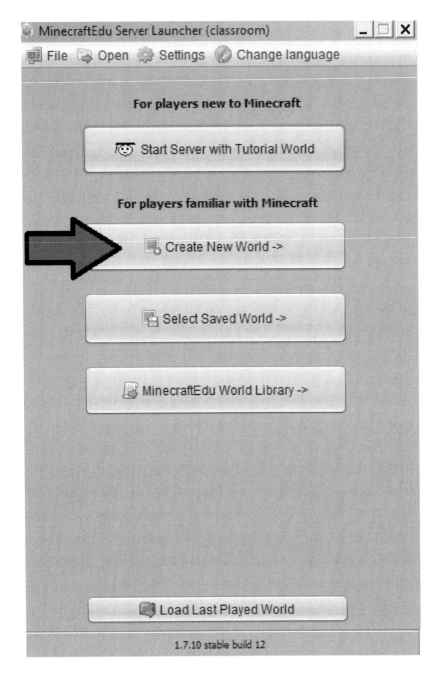

Step 3
Select the option to 'Generate a Completely Flat World'.

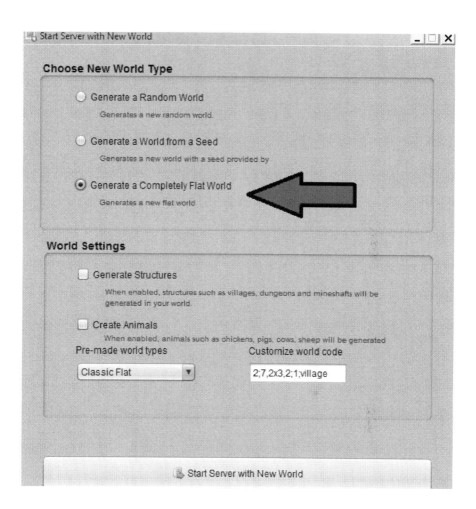

Step 4
Write the Server number on the whiteboard. (Students will need this for later.) Then, from the World Settings tab, make sure the game mode is set to 'Creative'. In creative mode, students have all the building blocks available that they will need to build.

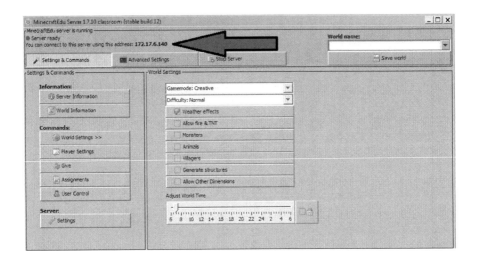

Step 5
Next, make sure that you set a teacher password (you will use this to enter the Minecraft the world as a teacher).

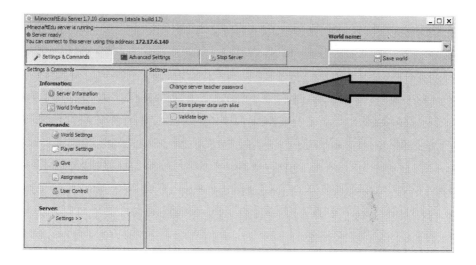

Step 6
Before students begin using Minecraft, make sure that you divide them into five teams:

Students in each of these construction teams should work together to create interesting rides and attractions for their theme park.

Student Instructions for Opening Minecraft:

Step 1. Open up Minecraft from the Start menu and select 'Start MinecraftEdu'.

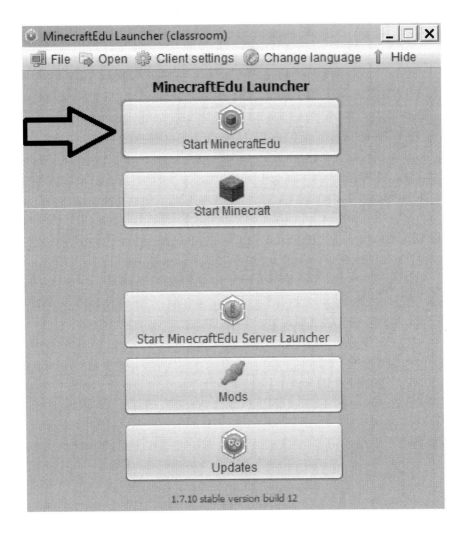

Step 2. Choose your player name (this should be your real name, so that your teacher can identify you in the Minecraft world) and select whether you are male or female.

Step 3. Select 'Multiplayer'.

Step 4. Click 'Direct Connect'.

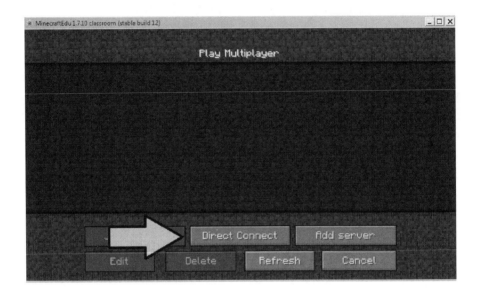

Step 5. Type in the Server number that your teacher has written on the whiteboard.

Activity

Once students enter the Minecraft world, they should get started straightaway with the task of building their city. This should last three lessons.

Some students may need extra support with learning how to use the controls. For these students, show them the basic controls to move around and select blocks for building.

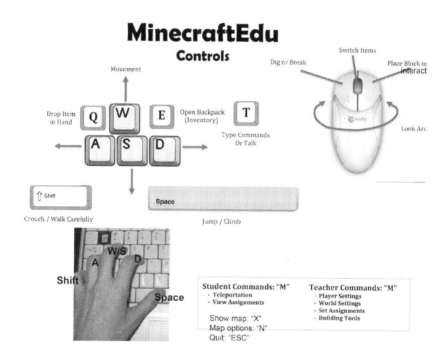

As a teacher, you can fly around the world to monitor students' progress.

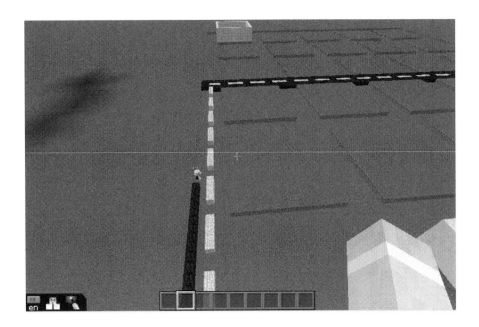

Before quitting Minecraft and closing the server, make sure that you save the Minecraft game from the Minecraft server window.

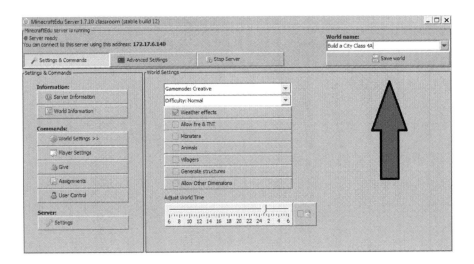

Plenary

Before finishing this theme park project in Minecraft, students should take screenshots of their Minecraft world in order to upload to their digital portfolio.

Year 5 - Robotics

Assessment focus areas: Computer Science & Information Technology

Beginning - **Must**	Developing – **Should**	Mastering - **Could**
Write programs that accomplish specific goals. Use sequence in programs.	Design programs that accomplish specific goals. Design and create program. Debug programs that accomplish specific goals. Use repetition in programs. Control or simulate physical systems. Use logical reasoning to detect and correct errors in programs. Understand how computer networks can provide multiple services, such as the world wide web. Appreciate how search results are selected.	Solve problems by decomposing them into smaller parts. Use selection in programs. Work with variables. Use logical reasoning to explain how some simple algorithms work. Use logical reasoning to detect and correct errors in algorithms.

Lesson 1 - Learn basic programming skills to control and orientate

Lesson 2 - Use Lego to build a robot

Lesson 3 - Follow instructions to build and test a Lego robot

Lesson 4 - Use software to program the Lego robot

Lesson 5 - Program the Lego robot to complete a complex sequence of movements

Lesson 1
Learn basic programming skills to control and orientate

Introduction
Use the interactive whiteboard to show the students how to access and use the Blockly Maze website: https://blockly-games.appspot.com/maze.

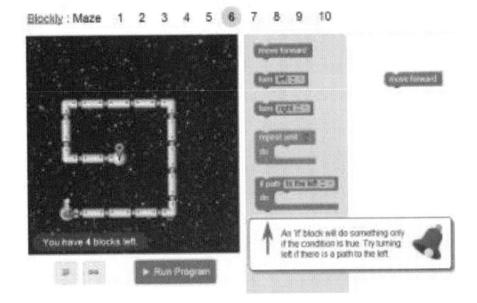

Demonstrate how to set to the Space scene by clicking on the settings in the top right-hand corner of the window:

Activity
Students should be challenged to achieve the highest level possible within the lesson time! They should save an image / screen capture of their progress and upload to their digital portfolios. Use the "snipping" tool:

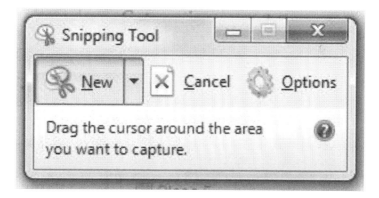

Plenary
Discuss any revelations, issues or problems which arose. How far did they get?

Lesson 2
Use Lego to build a robot

Introduction
Discuss space travel and exploration with the students, especially the dangers and difficulties for humans. What part can and do robots play in all of this? Talk about different uses of robots in space.

A recent example is Kirobo (http://www.space.com/21752-japan-launching-talking-robot-august.html), a talking Japanese robot which has gone to space as a companion to the astronauts. You can show the students this video (https://www.youtube.com/watch?v=xqShesZ3v-g) of Kirobo in space.

Activity
Students should be organised into six groups, designating themselves as **Director** (instruction reader), **Identifier** (Lego piece finder), **Constructor** (Lego builder) and

Project Manager (overseeing the whole group and ensuring progress).

This video can be shown (https://www.youtube.com/watch?v=fP2bgGj7hSs), which shows a stop motion of the robot being built. Students should write their names and jobs onto a piece of paper and attach this to their Lego box as they will be working on this project over the next few weeks. As soon as they are ready, they can start to build their robot. It is important to insist on tidy and highly organised group working skills – placing the pieces to be used on the lid, for example, and arranging all the other parts and components carefully within the box.

Plenary
Ensure that all the pieces are put away carefully – stress to the students that they cannot lose any of the material and that they will be returning to use the same set next lesson.

Lesson 3
Follow instructions to build and test a Lego robot

Introduction
Revise the overall reasons for this project – students are building a robot which they will then take to the computer lab to program so the robots are enabled and ready for a mission to Mars!

Activity
Students continue to build their robots. When it is done, they can test that it works by programming directly into the NX brick.

Plenary
Carefully store the finished robots with their names, ready to take to the computer lab for programming.

Lesson 4
Use software to program the Lego robot

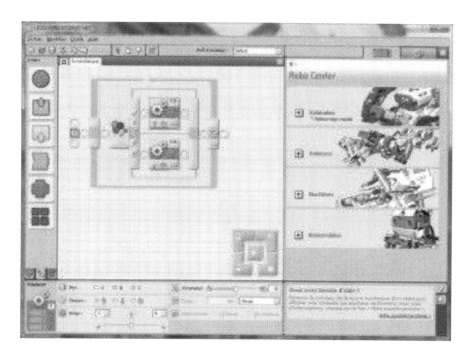

Introduction
Carefully take the students and their robots to the computer lab. Demonstrate the software, creating a sequence of actions and then saving your file. Plug in the brick and upload your program, then execute and watch what your robot does. Did it do what was intended? Does the programming need amendments?

Activity
Students should work individually at computers and all of them should save a program. Try to ensure all students have a go at uploading their program to a robot.

Plenary
Look at some of the more detailed programs and ask the creators to explain the steps and processes to the class.

Lesson 7
Program the Lego robot to complete a complex sequence of movements

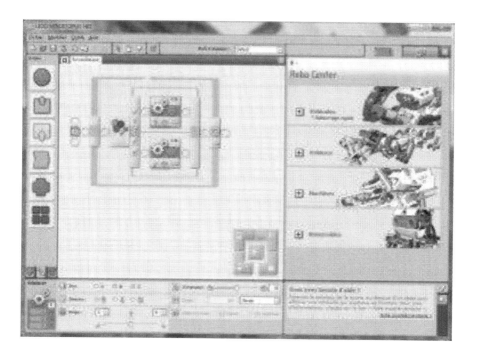

Introduction
In the classroom – can the students add a light sensor to their robot? In the computer lab with the robots – ask the students to include the light sensor in their programming. Use black tape to set up a "Mars Mission Maze" in the corridor. Can students write a program to enable their robots to complete the mission?

Activity
Students should work individually at computers and try to create a more complex program, including using the light sensor. They can test out their programs using the prepared "Mars Maze".

Plenary
Look at some of the more detailed programs and ask the creators to explain the steps and processes to the class.

Year 6 - E-Safety

Assessment focus area: Digital Literacy & Information Technology

Beginning (**Must**)	Developing (**Should**)	Mastering (**Could**)
Articulate rules to follow in order to stay safe online. Identify the rules to follow for computer & Internet use.	Identify and define spam, cyberbullying and viruses. Explain what netiquette means and how we can demonstrate good netiquette online.	Use WordArt to enhance Safer Internet displays.

Lesson 1: Learn rules to follow for computer & Internet use
Lesson 2: Identify the risks associated with using digital communication
Lesson 3: Recognise key hazards of using the Internet
Lesson 4: Demonstrate good netiquette

Lesson 1
Learn rules to follow for computer & Internet use

Introduction
Ask: what rules should we follow in the ICT lab? Elicit from the children that they should not rock on chairs, bring food or drink near the computers, etc.

Model writing some of these rules on a Google Slide, and show children how to upload this slide to the digital portfolio.

Activity
Using Google Classroom, provide each child with a copy of a blank Google Slide. They should use this slide to create their own display of rules to follow in the ICT lab, and then upload this to Google Classroom.

Plenary
Ask children to share their Google Slides with the rest of the class. Make sure that these are uploaded to the students' digital portfolios.

Lesson 2
Identify the risks associated with using digital communication

Introduction
Brainstorm with the children some of the risks associated with using the Internet, and show them the Consequences video located here:
https://www.youtube.com/watch?v=EQdyBpMvdJM

Discuss the mistakes that the girl (Jade) made. Elicit from the children that if we need to be careful what we share online, and this can be especially important with personal photos.

Activity
Using Google Classroom, provide each child with a blank Google Slide template. On the Google Slide, children should do the following:

- Record what digital communication technologies they use themselves.
- Write us some rules that Jade should follow to help her stay safe online in the future.

Plenary
Review what the children have learnt in this lesson. What are the risks associated with digital communication tools? How can we minimise these risks?

Lesson 3
Recognise key hazards of using the Internet, including spam, cyber-bullying and viruses

Introduction

Ask students what they understand by the terms virus, spam and cyber bullying. Elicit from students the following definitions:

- *Cyber bullying*: People sending unkind or nasty messages.
- *Spam*: A message trying to sell you products or persuade you to visit their website.
- *Virus*: A nasty program that can damage your computer and files on it.

Activity

Ask children to use the Sorted website (http://www.childnet.com/sorted/) to research up to ten facts about online safety. These facts should be presented on a Google Slide.

Plenary

Check children have included a range of facts such as:

- **the importance of checking email attachments are safe to open** (e.g. by confirming with the sender or using an anti-virus program like the free *Microsoft Security Essentials*);
- **the need to just delete any spam messages** as they are likely going to be unwanted adverts or messages asking you for personal information to claim a prize you've apparently won (which likely won't exist and your details will be used for fraudulent reasons/to send more spam instead);

- **to never agree to meet up with strangers you've only met online** in case they aren't who they say they are and you are put in a vulnerable position;
- **to always report incidents of cyberbullying immediately to a trusted adult**, keeping the received messages as proof/evidence and not responding to the bully with a nasty comment back (which makes you as bad as them).

Lesson 4
Demonstrate good netiquette

Introduction
Ask the children if anyone knows what etiquette means?
Explain that it just means we are polite with other people,
showing them respect. Ask: what do you think netiquette
means then? Elicit from the children that netiquette
refers to how we behave online.

Brainstorm with the children some ideas for good
netiquette, e.g. don't write all in capitals, re-read what
you write before you send it, ask permission before
posting things about friends, etc.

Activity
Ask children to produce a display using Google Docs,
outlining a set of rules for following good netiquette.
Encourage children to use Word Art (for their title: Insert
Drawing > Actions > WordArt)) and insert images. Once
finished and checked by the teacher, these displays can
be printed.

Plenary
Review the rules everyone has written for their display.
Are there any other rules that we can add? Why is it
important that we follow these rules?

Year 6 - Market Research

Assessment focus area: Digital Literacy & Information Technology

Beginning (**Must**)	Developing (**Should**)	Mastering (**Could**)
Create a set of good survey questions.	Work collaboratively to plan questions. Analyse the data obtained from a survey.	Present their research findings.

Lesson 1: Create a survey using Google forms
Lesson 2: Complete and enhance survey with images
Lesson 3 & 4: Collect and analyse the results of the survey
Lesson 5: Search for free to use or share images of houses
Lesson 6: Plan interviews

Lesson 1
Create a survey using Google forms

Introduction

Explain that market research means finding out information about the people who you are trying to get to buy your product. In a few weeks, students will be designing a dream home to sell, so they will need to find out what people look for when buying a home. Begin by asking: what is a survey? Elicit from the children that a survey is a way of finding out people's opinions by asking them questions.

In today's lesson, children will be making their own survey to find out about what would be the dream home of their classmates.

First, discuss what makes good survey questions, reminding children that survey questions should be simple and free from bias. Look at an example:

How fantastic do you think it is living on the top floor?

Compare this question with:

Would you prefer to live on the top floor of an apartment or the ground floor?

Ask: which question is more appropriate for a survey? Make sure everyone understands that the first question contains bias, as it is a leading question that encourages a certain answer. Survey questions should be balanced like the second question, ensuring that respondents will give a true answer rather than what they think you want to hear.

Model how to create a survey using Google Forms. (Go to Google Drive > click Create > More > Google Forms). The survey should contain at least 10 questions, and it should be sent to no more than 5 classmates. Remind students that there are legal and ethical reasons why they should not collect respondents' names.

For example:

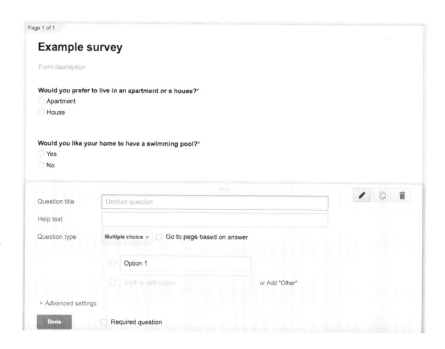

Explore the different questions types: multiple choice, checkboxes, linear scale and paragraph.

Activity
Using Google Forms, each child should create a survey that has at least 10 questions.

Plenary
Ask children to share some of the questions they have written. Make sure that the questions use the appropriate format, e.g. asking if the question should be multiple choice, checkbox or scale.
A question like "How important is it for you live in a city?" would best use a scale format rather than multiple choice.

Discuss these examples with the children. (These surveys do not need to be saved - they will save automatically).

Lesson 2
Complete and enhance survey with images

Introduction
Show children how to access the surveys that they were working on from the previous lesson (students should be able to access this from their Recent folder on the Google Drive).

Review appropriate survey questions. Then model how to insert pictures to appear next to the survey questions.

Activity
Children should insert pictures to appear next to their survey questions. Once students have finished, they should send their survey to five peers in their class. (As class teacher, you will need to allocate a list for each student of peers who students should send their survey to).

Plenary
Review examples of children's surveys, explaining that children will be sending these out next lesson.

Lesson 3 & 4
Collect and analyse the results of the survey

Introduction
In this lesson, students should send the survey have created to no more than 5 of their classmates to complete **(make sure that you have prepared a list for the children beforehand, which shows the names of classmates they should send their survey to - this will ensure that everyone receives an equal number of surveys)**.

Allow sufficient time for students to fill out the surveys they have received. Once all the children have finished filling out the surveys they have received, remind them of how to get an overview of responses to the surveys they created last lesson using the *Responses* > *Summary of responses* charts. Ask the students to take a screenshot of the graphs or other results to Google Slides for later use, writing notes about what they have learnt. (Show students how to make a screenshot by clicking together Cntrl + Prnt Scrn and the Cntrl + V in Paint ready to be cropped).

Here is an example of what a summary of responses might look like:

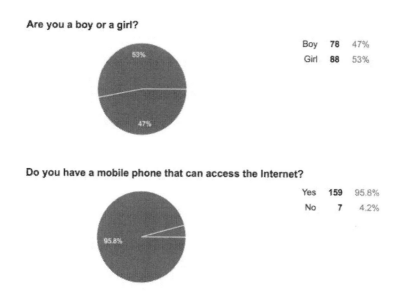

Are you a boy or a girl?

Boy	78	47%
Girl	88	53%

Do you have a mobile phone that can access the Internet?

Yes	159	95.8%
No	7	4.2%

Each pie chart should then be copied and pasted onto Google Slides - as shown by example below:

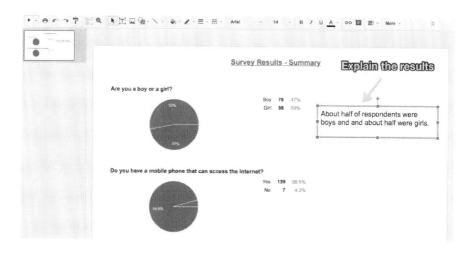

Lesson 5
Search for free to use or share images of houses

Introduction
Explain to students that in order to help them with their design ideas, they should search for other dream homes on the Internet. Explain that they will need to perform a Google Advanced Image Search - model how to do this, selecting images that are free to use or share.

This is because many images on the Internet are protected by copyright - show children the copyright video (https://www.youtube.com/watch?v=APuwNPI4-EE) to remind them of why we search for Royalty Free images.

Activity
Students should search for at least five images of "dream homes", which are Royalty Free - i.e. free to use or share. They should upload these images to their digital portfolios.

Plenary
Using NetSupport School, review with the children some examples of their portfolio pages, which show images of dream homes. Ask the children how these images have helped them with their own design ideas.

Lesson 6
Plan interviews

Introduction
Discuss with the children how they can find more detailed information about what people are looking for in a dream home. Elicit from the children that they could use questionnaires. Explain that in today's lesson, children will be working in groups of five to create a questionnaire of no more than five questions. In each group, one person should be a representative to answer another group's interview questions. Discuss the sort of questions they could ask as part of their questionnaire.

Activity
In groups of five, children work on a shared Google Doc to write down five questions for their questionnaire. Each group member should draft a few possible ideas into the collaborative document, and then as a group they should decide on how to refine these. When they have completed the questionnaire, they should copy and paste this onto their individual Google Slides made in the previous lesson. When they have done this, they can request to interview one member (the representative) from another group. They should write up key notes from the interview on their individual Google Slides.

Plenary
Check that all the groups have written up the questionnaires and everybody has written down notes from these interviews on their Google Slide.

Year 6 - 3D Modelling

Assessment focus area: Digital Literacy & Information Technology

Beginning (**Must**)	Developing (**Should**)	Mastering (**Could**)
Create a basic design on a spreadsheet. Using some (but not all) formatting features. Make a basic design in Google Drawing.	Correctly format cells on a spreadsheet (change size of cells, add borders, change colour of cells and merge cells, where appropriate). Upload completed work to the digital portfolio.	Use Sketchup to design a 3D model of a home. Take screenshot of the 3D model in Sketchup to upload onto the digital portfolio.

Lesson 1 - Design the interior of your ideal home using Google Sheets
Lesson 2 - Use Google Drawings to design the outside of your ideal home
Lesson 3 & 4 - Use Sketchup to design a 3D model of your ideal home
Lesson 5 - Format cells in spreadsheets
Lesson 6 - Use Google Sheets to calculate the costs of building your ideal home

Lesson 1
Design the interior of your ideal home using Google Sheets

Introduction

Remind children of the work they did using Google Sheets. Explain that they will be using Google Sheets to design the interior of some of the rooms in their ideal homes. You can show them a readymade example like this:

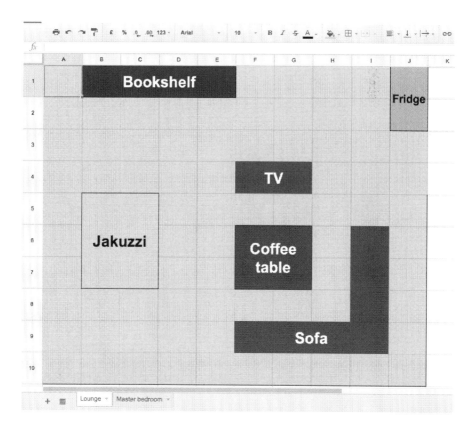

Model how to make an interior design, beginning with a 10 x 10 grid. Show children how to make all the cells the same size, add borders, change colours of cells and merge cells, where appropriate. Then show them how labels of the different pieces of furniture can be added. Ask children to begin designing one of the rooms in their ideal home, for example, the lounge.

Activity
Students should begin by accessing Google Sheets. They will begin by creating a grid, which represents the first room. (The grid does not have to be 10 x 10 but it should be a realistic size). All the appropriate furniture should be added to the grid. As an extension, children can continue adding new tabs to the spreadsheet to create additional designs of new rooms.

When they have finished a few designs, ask children to upload the finished room design spreadsheet to their digital portfolio.

Plenary
Using NetSupport, review some of the designs that the children made. Was everyone able to merge cells, add borders, etc. correctly?

Lesson 2
Use Google Drawings to design the outside of your ideal home

Introduction
Show children how to access Google Drawings (Google Drive > New > More > Google Drawings). Explain that they will be using Google Drawings to design the outside of their ideal home - you can show them an example like this:

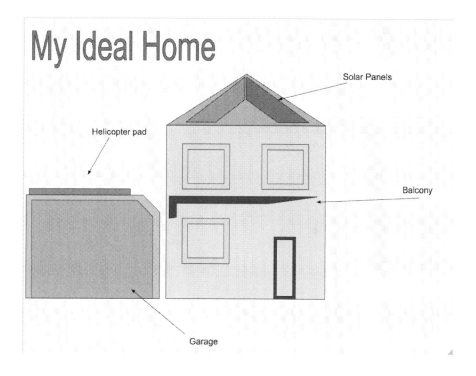

The drawing should include different coloured shapes, labels of key features and a title using WordArt.

Activity
Students go ahead and create a design of their digital home. When the design is finished, it should be uploaded to the students´ digital portfolio.

Plenary
Check work submitted so far on the digital portfolios. Has everyone been able to upload their Google Drawing?

Lesson 3 & 4
Use Sketchup to design a 3D model of your ideal home

Introduction
Show children the tutorial video for making a virtual house in Sketchup located here:
https://www.youtube.com/watch?v=wM8mOZTQPwY.

Explain that students will spend the next two lessons making some of the rooms for their ideal home - the only limit in what they can accomplish is their imagination! If you have access to a 3D printer, offer to 3D print the best designs!

Activity
Students design the 3D homes. Encourage them not to spend too much time on small details - the most important thing is to get an idea of what the home would look like. They should take some screenshots of their work to display on their digital portfolios.

Extension Activity
Can the students see any tools that might allow them to add colour and texture to their finished buildings? Can they find some ways to fill the buildings with realistic building materials such as bricks, roofing tiles and glass?

Plenary
Display some of the students' work for the rest of the class to see. What are the common features of these ideal homes? How could they be improved?

Lesson 5
Format cells in spreadsheets

Introduction
In order to consolidate children's learning of spreadsheets and design, we will play battleships. Show the students the video here to get started:
https://www.youtube.com/watch?v=ToZ6vhCiF_s&feature=youtube_gdata

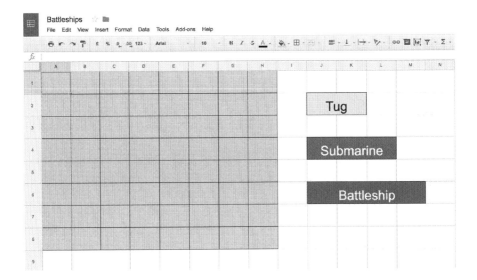

Activity
Children create their 10 x 10 battleship grid in Google Sheets and add three vessels onto the grid.

Plenary
Call out different cell references. If a student has a vessel within the range of the cell reference you have just called, then that part of their vessel gets destroyed and they should colour it in black.

Lesson 6
Use Google Sheets to calculate the costs of building your ideal home

Introduction
Explain to the children that before a home can be built for real, the total costs need to be calculated. In this lesson, we will be using spreadsheets to calculate the costs of all the materials that you will need for your ideal home based on designs from the previous lesson.

Using the 'Building Materials Cost Spreadsheet' template, tell the children to imagine, for simplicity, that there is a set cost for building each room in their ideal home. Demonstrate calculating all the costs for building materials using formulae. Tell the children to imagine that they have a different budget for each room, so will need to keep in budget.

Note for teacher: Create a 'Building Materials Cost Analysis' template as illustrated in this example below. The layout and numbers can be adapted as you see fit. The important thing is to demonstrate using formulae to calculate all the costs for building a restaurant.

£   %   .0   .00   123 ▾   Arial   ▾   10   ▾   **B**   *I*   -S-   A ▾   ◇ ▾   ⊞ ▾

fx   Building Materials Cost Analysis

	A	B	C	D	E	F
1	**Building Materials Cost Analysis**					
2						
3	Number of bedrooms to be built:		5			
4						
5	Material	Price (per unit)	Number of units needed	Cost		
6	Concrete	40	10	2000		
7	Electrics	60	5	1500		
8	Glass	70	6	2100		
9	Metal	80	8	3200		
10	Wood	50	5	1250		
11	Plaster	45	4	900		
12	Plumbing	70	3	1050		
13						
14						
15						
16			Total	12000		
17			Budget	25000		
18			Change	13000		
19						
20						
21						

Activity

Based on the children's design specifications (e.g. perhaps they have decided to have a given number of bedrooms and bathrooms), they should begin calculating the total cost of building each set of rooms. To do this, share with students the Building Materials Cost Analysis as a template using Google Classroom, making sure each child has his or her own copy. When students have finished this spreadsheet and calculated the total cost and budget remaining, they should embed the spreadsheet into their digital portfolio.

Plenary

Review children's answers. Did anyone go over their budget allocation? If they did, discuss how they would need to take out loans to cover their costs. If they still have money left in their budget, discuss how they could best spend the money.

Year 6 - Scratch

Assessment focus areas: Digital Literacy & Information Technology

Beginning - **Must**	Developing - **Should**	Mastering - **Could**
Complete coding activities from Kahn Academy website independently. Design the character and setting for an animation using the Scratch interface.	Create a simple maze game in Scratch, following the example provided.	Develop the maze game to include sound effects, a point system and a new level.

Lesson 1: Introduction to Computer Science
Lesson 2: Introduction to Scratch
Lesson 3: Make a sprite and a background
Lesson 4 & 5: Making your own Scratch game

Lesson 1
Introduction to Computer Science

Introduction
Explain to the children that they will be learning how to code for the next several lessons. Begin by showing them the Hour of Code video: https://www.khanacademy.org/computing/hour-of-code/hour-of-code-tutorial/v/anybody-can-learn-code.

Activity
After watching the video, children should continue using this site on their own to complete the coding challenges.
(Optional - children to printscreen and paste into a Google doc each time they create the different tasks - this can be used for assessment evidence.)

Plenary
Review how everybody got on. Next lesson students will begin building their own game using the skills they have learnt in this lesson.

Lesson 2
Introduction to Scratch

Introduction
Introduce children to Scratch by showing them an example of an animation built in Scratch:
https://scratch.mit.edu/projects/69535782/

Show them "inside" the animation, pointing out that it is made up of code. Demonstrate altering a part of the code, explaining how this affects the game.

Activity
In this lesson, children should set up their Scratch accounts **(make sure that they write down their usernames and passwords - and they should email you with these details!)**
Children should then try to create their own simple animation using Scratch in which a sprite is controlled using the arrow keys.

Plenary
Discuss with the children what they think makes a good game.

Lesson 3
Make a sprite and a background

Introduction
Explain to children that they will be building a game, which features an endangered animal. Show children this example of the type of game that you would like them to build:
https://scratch.mit.edu/projects/69535782/

Over the next few lessons, students will build a similar game, involving an endangered animal inside a maze.

Ask: what is a sprite? The sprite is our character or any graphical object, which is controlled by the code. In this game, the main sprite is the mouse. Can children see any other sprites in the game?

Demonstrate how to make a sprite and a game background using the paint function in Scratch.

Activity
Children make their main sprite and background. As an extension, they will need to make other sprites that their main sprite will interact with, e.g. a mousetrap, a door, etc.

As an extension, students can begin watching Part 1 video tutorial for building their maze game
https://www.youtube.com/watch?v=du4LJWxcrck

Plenary
Look at examples of children's work to showcase to the rest of the class. What makes a particularly good sprite or background?

Lesson 4 & 5
Making your own Scratch game

Introduction
Ask children to log into their Scratch accounts and complete the Maze tutorial:
https://scratch.mit.edu/projects/2825901/.

In addition, share via Google Classroom the tutorial videos for students to access as they are building their game:

Part 1 (https://www.youtube.com/watch?v=du4LJWxcrck)
Part 2 (https://www.youtube.com/watch?v=uX--NIhKr4w)
Part 3 (https://www.youtube.com/watch?v=4bUsug56OdQ)

Activity
Children should make their own Scratch game based on the concept of a maze in which the main sprite starts at the beginning again if he touches the walls of the maze.

Plenary
Children can think-pair-share, playing one another's games to see what works well and what could be improved.

Year 6 - Building a City (Minecraft)

Assessment focus areas: Digital Literacy & Information Technology

Beginning (**Must**)	Developing (**Should**)	Mastering (**Could**)
Insert text and images into a Google Slide. Define and identify the differences between commercial, industrial, municipal, public services and residential buildings. Control and navigate an avatar in a Minecraft world.	Navigate Google Maps and take screenshots of different cities from an aerial view. Correctly format cells on a spreadsheet to represent the map of a city. Build different structures in Minecraft appropriate to the assigned construction group.	Make logical decisions about where to locate different buildings in the Minecraft world. Explain these decisions on the digital portfolio alongside relevant screenshots.

Lesson 1 - Create a presentation about cities around the world
Lesson 2 - Design the layout of a city using spreadsheets
Lesson 3, 4 & 5 - Use Minecraft to create a city
Lesson 6 - Explore and take screenshots of a city in Minecraft

Lesson 1
Create a presentation about cities around the world

Introduction
Students will use Google Maps (https://www.google.co.uk/maps/) to find different cities around the world. Model how to navigate Google Maps (by searching for different cities), and invite volunteers to demonstrate how to use the program. Once students have found a city in Google Maps, they should take a screenshot and upload this image to a Google Slide presentation.

Activity
Students to create a Google Slide, which features five different cities from around the world. This should include a title page, "Cities Around the World". Each slide should contain at least two images of the city (one of which should be a screenshot from Google Maps showing an aerial view of the city). At least three interesting facts should be written about the city next to the images.

London

- London is in the southeast of England.

- It is the biggest city in Europe.

- The tallest building in London is the Canary Wharf Tower.

When students have finished this presentation, it should be embedded into their digital portfolio.

Plenary
Ask for volunteers to present what they have learnt about different cities around the world. Do students notice any similarities between the cities they have looked at based on the aerial screenshots they have taken - e.g. plenty of roads and transport links, usually close to the sea, etc.

Lesson 2
Design the layout of a city using spreadsheets

Introduction

Explain that before students can begin to build their city using Minecraft, they must first design the city's layout using Google Sheets. Make sure that you share beforehand a 'city design template' via Google Classroom similar to the example below:

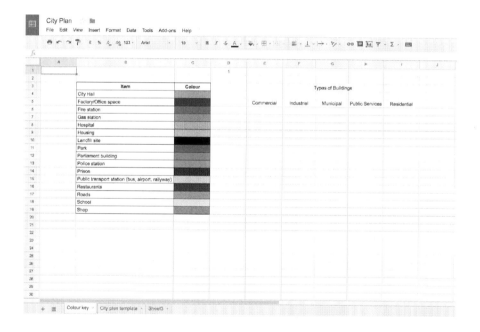

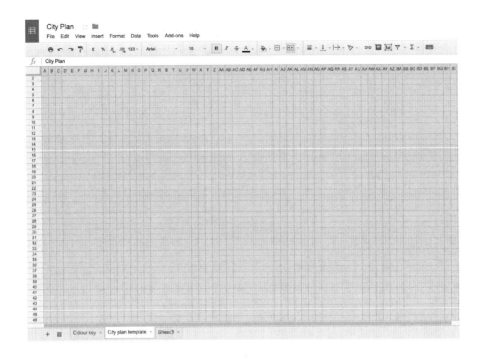

Demonstrate how to create the landscape design of a city:

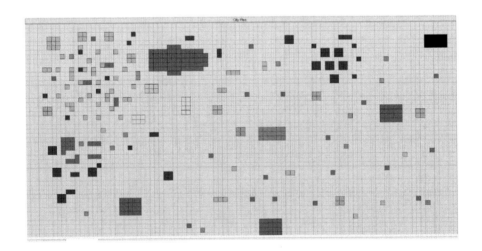

Explain that this design template example is not yet finished. Cross reference with the colour key sheet, and ask students to identify some of the different buildings based on the colour of the cells. Ask: what is missing from this design? (answer: roads)

Next lesson students will be working in groups according to different construction projects. Make sure that students are familiar with these different categories for buildings:

Commercial - buildings used to sell goods & services (e.g. shops)
Industrial - buildings used to make products (e.g. factories)
Municipal - buildings used by the government (e.g. parliament)
Public Services - buildings and infrastructure provided for use by the public (e.g. roads)
Residential - buildings that provide people with a place to live (e.g. apartments)

Activity

Using the city design template, students should follow the colour key to design the layout of their city.

On the colour key tab, students should also complete the table, writing up which buildings belong to which category:

Commercial	Industrial	Municipal	Public Services	Residential
Gas station	Factory	City Hall	Fire station	Housing
Restaurant		Parliament	Hospital	
Shop			Landfill site	
Cinema			Park	
			Police station	
			Prison	
			Bus station	
			Roads	
			Roads	
			Schools	

Once they have finished, students should upload this design to their digital portfolio.

Plenary

Use NetSupport to showcase some of the students' designs. Discuss the locations where students have decided to put their buildings. For example, discuss why it might not be a good idea to put a prison or landfill site near a school or residential area. Where would it be best to put parks? Students will need to think carefully about the location of their buildings for next lesson, as they will be working together to build their city in Minecraft.

Lesson 3, 4 & 5
Use Minecraft to create a city

Introduction
Explain to the students that during this unit, they will be
working together to build a virtual city, using Minecraft. Note -
some students will be very familiar with Minecraft, so it will be
their job to help support students to help their classmates.

Teacher Instructions for Opening Minecraft:

Step 1
Open the Minecraft Server Tool on the teacher computer and
select 'Start MinecraftEdu Server Launcher'.

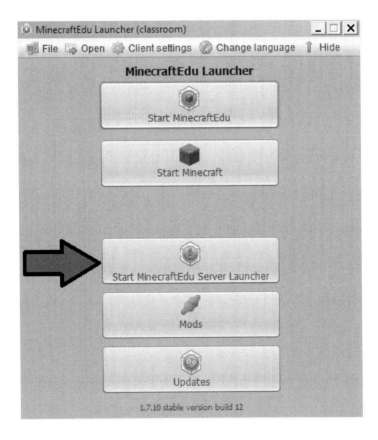

Step 2
Click 'Create New World'.

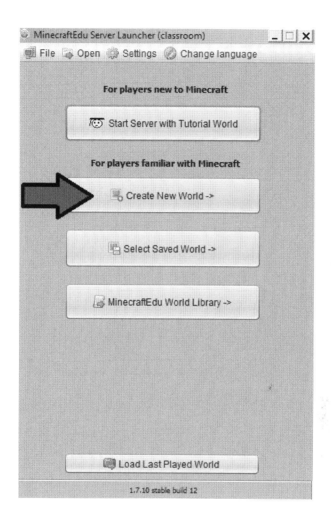

Step 3
Select the option to 'Generate a Completely Flat World'.

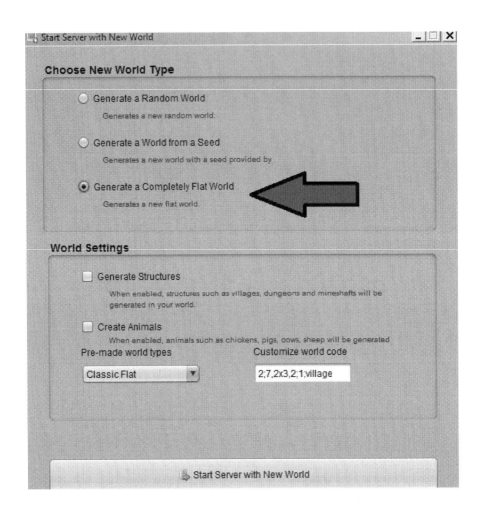

Step 4

Write the Server number on the whiteboard. (Students will need this for later.) Then, from the World Settings tab, make sure the game mode is set to 'Creative'. In creative mode, students have all the building blocks available that they will need to build.

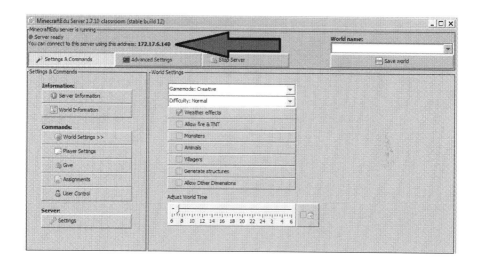

Step 5
Next, make sure that you set a teacher password (you will use this to enter the Minecraft the world as a teacher).

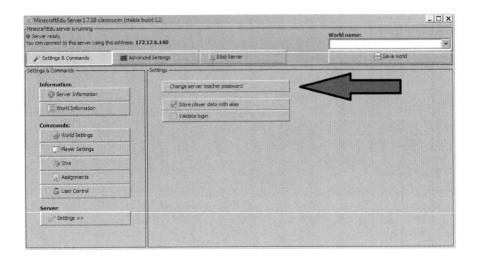

Step 6
Before students begin using Minecraft, make sure that you divide them into five teams:

Commercial	Industrial	Municipal	Public Services	Residential

Remind students of the different buildings associated with each category. Students in each of these construction teams will be making buildings appropriate to their category, e.g. students in the Commercial construction team will build shops, restaurants, etc.

Student Instructions for Opening Minecraft:

Step 1. Open Minecraft from the Start menu and select 'Start MinecraftEdu'.

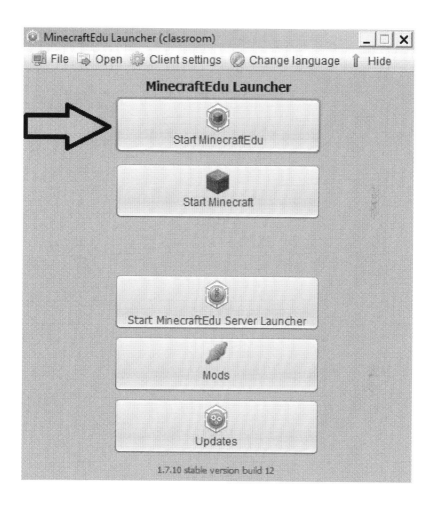

Step 2. Choose your player name (this should be your real name, so that your teacher can identify you in the Minecraft world) and select whether you are male or female.

Step 3. Select 'Multiplayer'.

Step 4. Click 'Direct Connect'.

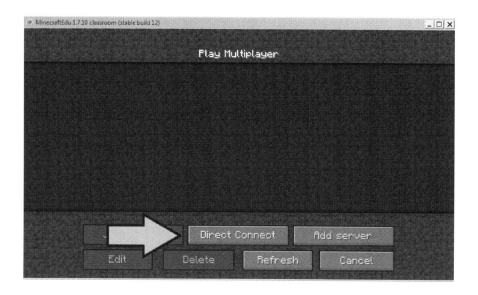

Step 5. Type in the Server number that your teacher has written on the whiteboard.

Activity

Once students enter the Minecraft world, they should get started straightaway with the task of building their city. This should last three lessons.

Some students may need extra support with learning how to use the controls. For these students, show them the basic controls to move around and select blocks for building.

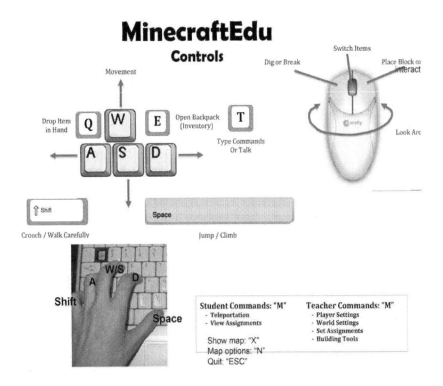

As a teacher, you can fly around the world to monitor students' progress.

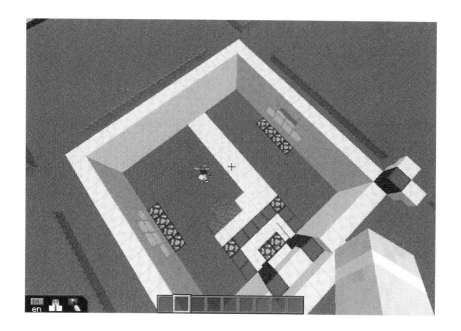

Before quitting Minecraft and closing the server, make sure that you save the Minecraft game from the Minecraft server window.

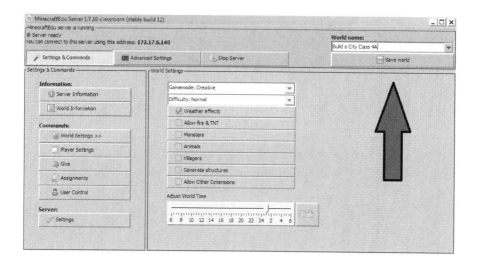

Plenary

Before finishing this Build a City project in Minecraft, students should take screenshots of their Minecraft world in order to upload to their digital portfolio.

Lesson 6
Explore and take screenshots of a city in Minecraft

Introduction
In this lesson, students will explore a readymade city. From the MinecraftEdu launcher window, click 'Saved worlds' and click 'Typical City'. Explain to students that they will need to take at least five different screenshots in this city to record different types of buildings according to the following five categories:

Commercial
Industrial
Municipal
Public Services
Residential

Each screenshot should then be uploaded to the student's digital portfolio. Show students an example of one made earlier:

Commercial - Shopping Mall

Industrial - Factory

Municipal - City Hall

Public Services - Hospital

Activity
Students explore the city you have loaded and take screenshots as explained in the introduction. As an extension, students can construct additional buildings.

Optional:
As a fun exit point activity, explain that students will need to fortify their city against a zombie attack. They will have just 10 minutes to build their fortifications and protect the city after which time you will change the game mode from creative to survival.

Plenary
Discuss which screenshots the students had taken. Check that everyone was able to correctly identify the different types of buildings in the city according to the five categories: commercial, industrial, public services, municipal and residential.

Year 6 - Geometry & Art

Assessment focus areas: Digital Literacy & Information Technology

Beginning (**Must**)	Developing (**Should**)	Mastering (**Could**)
Use a digital camera responsibly. Draw shapes using image creation software.	Use a digital tablet appropriately to create a portrait and cityscape. Take photographs of tessellations in the local environment and upload these to a digital portfolio. Use image creation software to draw tessellations. Create basic shapes using Scratch. Correctly resize and merge shapes in Tinkercad.	Develop new and creative 3D designs using Tinkercad. Print this design using the 3D printer. Be able to digitally edit photographs and make appropriate comments on the digital portfolio. Begin to develop complex geometric patterns using Scratch.

Lesson 1 - Develop skills to use a digital tablet for drawing
Lesson 2 - Use digital tablet to design a cityscape
Lesson 3 - Use Tinkercad to design your own 3D model
Lesson 4 - Program art in Scratch

Lesson 1
Develop skills to use a digital tablet for drawing

Introduction

Explain to students that they will begin this unit by learning about how to use digital tablets. These are tablets designed to replace the use of a mouse for drawing.

In this lesson, students will be creating a digital portrait. Show students this video to help get them started:
https://www.youtube.com/watch?v=GuhtGTeN76Q

To help students with this task, you can send them a photo to use as a stencil, e.g.
https://upload.wikimedia.org/wikipedia/commons/f/f1/BarackObamaportrait.jpg

Demonstrate opening up ArtRage Lite that students will be using with their digital tablet. Select the 'Tracing' button and show how to insert the image of Obama as a stencil.

Activity

Following the suggestions made in the video, students should experiment with their digital tablet to create a portrait.

Plenary
Review students' drawings. Which tools produced the best effects? What techniques did students find that helped them to make their drawing?

Lesson 2
Use digital tablet to design a cityscape

Introduction
In this lesson, students will create a digital drawing of a cityscape. Begin by showing students some different examples of cityscapes, and make sure that you share the links to these images via Google Classroom:

London
https://uaem2015london.files.wordpress.com/2015/01/panoramic_cityscapes4.jpg

Rio
https://images3.alphacoders.com/230/230357.jpg

Shanghai
https://userscontent2.emaze.com/images/47bc94df-1b3b-
4f90-b58b-
f51259277402/b607278620a3a03b1b64677d3cefb468.jpg

Show students this video about how to draw cityscapes:
https://www.youtube.com/watch?v=jcuIYUVzEP0

Activity
As in the previous lesson, students can insert a cityscape image to trace by clicking on the tracing button.

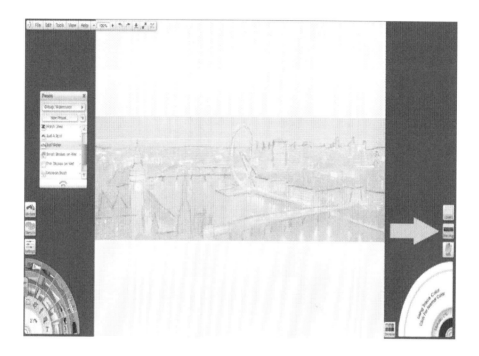

When students have finished tracing, they can right click on the tracing button, and click clear tracing image. Once this is done, students can focus on the painting of their cityscape.

Demonstrate the use of the watercolour brush, and select the "unclean brush" preset.

Plenary
Students who have finished their cityscapes should print their work to present for the rest of the class.

Lesson 3
Use Tinkercad to design your own 3D model

Introduction
If students have not acquired the basic skills for using Tinkercad (www.tinkercad.com), recap on these lessons from the Year 5 unit, 3D Modelling. If students already have experience of using Tinkercad, they are free to begin developing their own designs. Set students the competition of creating a small 3D model that roughly fits inside the following dimensions: 30mm x 30mm x 30mm. The best design from the class will be 3D printed! Show students a couple of examples, which have been 3D printed already. Let students hold these 3D printed models and pass them around the class. Emphasise that the 3D printer will do a better job at printing a small, simple 3D design than one that is overly complex. (For example, small letter fonts do not tend to print very well.)

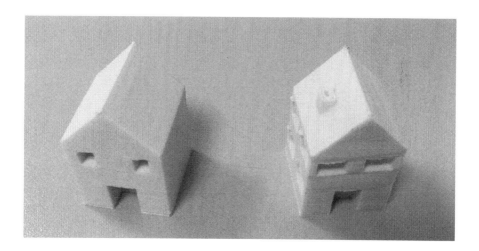

Activity
Using the same login details from the previous lesson, students should go ahead with their 3D designs. These will save automatically.

Plenary
At the end of the lesson, review the designs that students have made. (These will be visible under 'Projects' on the design homepage.)

Lesson 4
Program art in Scratch

Introduction

Explain to the students that they are going to use Scratch to create some art. Ask: what is a tessellation? Explain that a tessellation is art made up shapes closely fitted together. Begin by showing how Scratch has been used to create some tessellations based on Escher's work: https://scratch.mit.edu/projects/16643705/

In this lesson, students will be using some code to draw basic shapes (using the offline version of Scratch). First, shrink the Scratch cat (to about the size of the cursor) and demonstrate how to create a shape, using the following code:

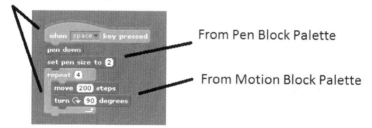

Based on the code above, ask students if they can anticipate what shape will be created when the spacebar is pressed - then show students the result.

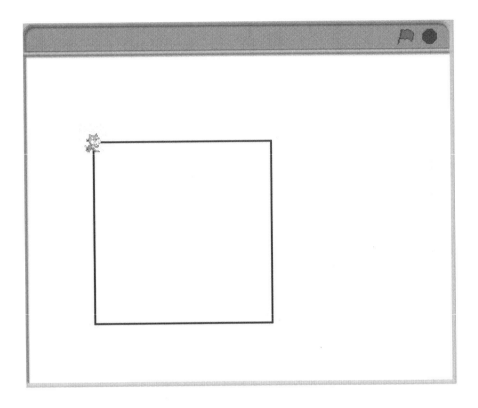

See if students can work out how to clear the drawing that has just been made. Elicit code similar to below:

You can also show how to make this design more interesting by using some of Scratch's other graphics functions, such as set pen colour, shade and size on the pen palette.

Next, see if students can come up with code to make an equilateral triangle:

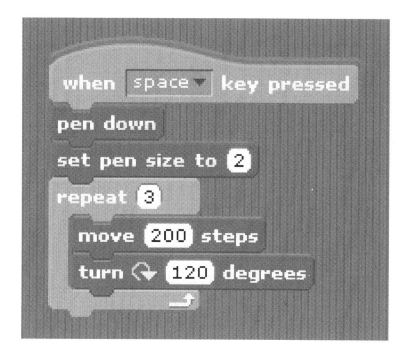

It may be necessary to remind students what an exterior angle is - the angle between any side of a shape and the line extended from the next side - point this out with the example of the equilateral triangle:

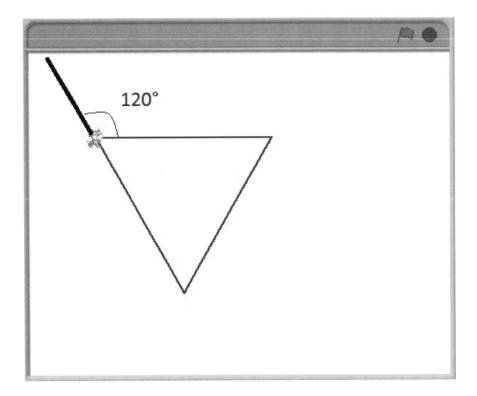

Finally, point out how to make the shape turn to create a spiralling pattern using another repeat loop and adding a "turn 5 degrees" block:

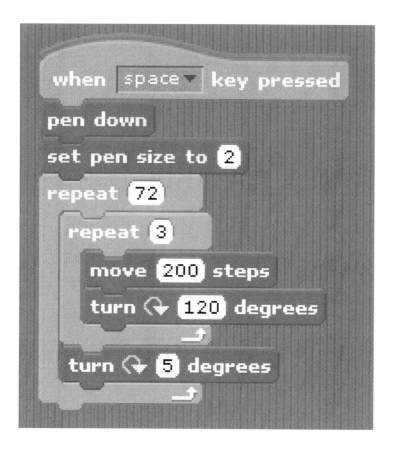

Activity
Ask students to draw some basic shapes in Scratch, such as equilateral triangles and squares. As an extension, they should create complex geometric patterns by repeatedly drawing a single shape then turning through a set angle.

In Google Classroom, post these links to Scratch projects that students can use to help with their ideas:
https://scratch.mit.edu/projects/16643705/
https://scratch.mit.edu/projects/52122722/

Plenary

Students should take screenshots of their Scratch work and upload these images to their digital portfolios with commentary.

Year 6 - Tutorial Video

Assessment focus areas: Digital Literacy & Information Technology

Beginning (**Must**)	Developing (**Should**)	Mastering (**Could**)
Use a screencasting software to record video output from a computer.	Make appropriate edits to the screencast using a movie editing program.	Add music to the video and a credits page.

Lesson 1 - Use screencasting software to make a tutorial video

Lesson 2 & 3 - Import screencast video into MoviePlus and make edits

Lesson 4 - Add background music to the tutorial video

Lesson 1
Use screencasting software to make a tutorial video

Introduction
Explain that in this lesson we will be learning how to do something called 'screencasting'. Does anyone know what a screencast is? Elicit that a screencast is simply a digital recording of the computer screen output. Screencasts are usually used in tutorial videos, which show us how to use a particular application.

Watch an example of a screencast video with students (https://www.youtube.com/watch?v=wM8mOZTQPwY). Discuss what worked well about this video and what could be improved. Ask students to make their own screencast video (using screencast-o-matic) about one of these three applications they have been learning to use this year (e.g. Sketchup, Tinkered or Scratch). Briefly demonstrate for students how to use screencast-o-matic to record using one of these applications.

Activity
Students use one of the applications (Sketchup, Tinkercad or Scratch) and should record a 5-minute screencast that demonstrates how to use the software or a particular function within the software. Students should make sure their video is saved in their student folder for next lesson.

As an extension, students can begin downloading the video into MoviePlus for the purpose of editing.

Plenary
Watch a couple of example screencasts that the students have made. Discuss steps for next lesson - importing the screencast video into MoviePlus and adding subtitles.

Lesson 2 & 3
Import screencast video into MoviePlus and make edits

Introduction
In this lesson, students will import their screencast video footage into MoviePlus and make necessary edits. These edits should include the addition of subtitles, transition slides and a credits page. (Explain that we will use subtitles rather than a voiceover because of the issue with background noise.)

Open MoviePlus and show students how to import their video footage into the program. Then demonstrate how to add slide transitions (click "Galleries") and subtitles (click "Insert Text").

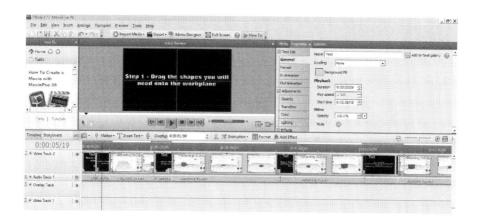

Activity
Students go ahead with importing their screencast video into MoviePlus and making the necessary edits, including the use of subtitles. When finished, students should download their completed work (click "Export" > "File" > "MP4" > "Next" > "Finish") as a video file and upload to their Google Drive.

Plenary

Invite students to share their videos with you via Google Drive, then choose examples to watch together as a class.

Lesson 4
Add background music to the tutorial video

Introduction
Ask students what could be done to make their videos more engaging to watch. Elicit that adding a soft background music can be an effective way of holding the listener's attention. However, it is important to respect copyright and choose music that has a Creative Commons licence, which means it is free to use and share.

Introduce students to the Free Music Archive (http://freemusicarchive.org/), a popular website dedicated to providing people with music licenced under Creative Commons.

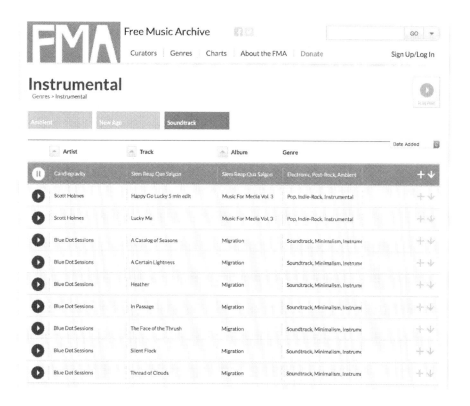

Explore an example of music together with the students and show how to download this as a file on the computer by clicking on the down facing arrow on the far right. Once the music is downloaded, demonstrate how to upload and add this to the tutorial video in MoviePlus. (Click "Import Media" > "Import"). Remind students that it is important to add a credits page at the end of the video, which states the name of the music and its composer.

Activity
Allow students time to explore and choose music from the Free Music Archive for use on their tutorial video. Once included in the video, students should add a credits page as well, including information about the name of the music used and the composer. Students should then save and reupload this new version of their tutorial video to Google Drive.

Plenary
Once again, invite students to share their videos with you via Google Drive, and then choose examples to watch together as a class. Discuss the difference that adding background music can make to the video.

Glossary of Key Terms

Algorithm – A precise step by step set of instructions used for a computer program.

Application – A program that performs a specific job for its users. For example, Microsoft Word is a program that enables users to type documents.

Browser – A piece of software that enables a user to surf the world wide web.

Computation – Performing a calculation by executing the instructions of a program on a computational device.

Digital device – A computer device, for example, a Bee-Bot, that performs a job for its users.

Computational thinking – The ability to analyse ways to solve problems using appropriate instructions, taking account of all possible solutions.

Computer science – The scientific study of instructions (algorithms) used to run computer applications and hardware.

Data – Information which can be stored, retrieved and changed in digital form using digital devices.

Debug – To find, remove and / or change errors in computer programming.

Digital citizenship – Appropriate and responsible use of digital technology.

Digital content – Images, videos, text or data, or a combination of these, which are made on a digital device.

Digital literacy – The ability to use and evaluate digital content, understanding the implications of its creation and distribution.

E-safety – Understanding and applying rules to protect against the risks to personal safety and privacy of personal information when using digital devices of all kinds.

Hardware – Physical items of computers such as desktop monitors, printers and scanners.

Input – The data that a computer receives.

Internet – A global network of computers linked together, allowing the exchange of data.

Operating system – The program that enables the computer to start and access different sorts of software on the computer, for example Microsoft Windows or iOS.

Output – The data that a computer sends.

Program / code (verb) – To create or modify a computer program.

Program / code (noun) – A sequence of instructions for a computer, written in an appropriate programming language.

Programming language – A formal language for representing statements, or commands, and data values used in a computer program.

Sequence – A number of program statements, to be carried out one after another.

Software – The programs that enable computers to undertake specific functions. Common web browsing software for example, includes Internet Explorer, Google Chrome and Safari.

Variable – In programming, a variable is a value in the code for a program that can be changed.

For more information on Computing and ICT Lessons for children, visit **technologyforlearners.com**.

Printed in Great Britain
by Amazon